Gut Feelings

Gut Feelings

A Writer's Truths and Minute Inventions

Merrill Joan Gerber

THE UNIVERSITY OF WISCONSIN PRESS

The University of Wisconsin Press
1930 Monroe Street
Madison, Wisconsin 53711

www.wisc.edu/wisconsinpress/

3 Henrietta Street
London WC2E 8LU, England

1   3   5   4   2

Printed in the United States of America

Library of Congress Cataloging-in-Publication Data
Gerber, Merrill Joan.
Gut feelings: a writer's truths and minute inventions / Merrill Joan Gerber.
p.   cm.
Includes bibliographical references.
ISBN 0-299-18350-5 (alk. paper)
1. Gerber, Merrill Joan.
2. Authors, American—20th century—Biography.
3. Fiction—Authorship.   I. Title.
PS3557.E664 Z463   2003
813'.54—dc21   2002010202

This book is dedicated with love to my women friends
who write, who read, who study, who paint;
women who support me, who lift me up
and who are the most astute readers I know—
Katerine Gaja, Joan Givner, Susan Koppelman, Jenijoy La Belle,
Nancy Levinson, Cynthia Ozick, Lynn Ross,
and Charlotte Zoe Walker

∞

To my students—
Lesley Dahl, Joan Fry, Cathie Sandstrom Smith, Madeleine Swift,
and Cherry Jean Vasconcellos

∞

To my book club—
Cecilia Fox, Elaine Gaynor, Miriam Kranser,
Pearl Weinstein Tyree, Evelyn Robinson, Beverly Sloane,
Evelyn Speiser, and Connie Taus

Contents

Preface

The Form in the Stone—Some Notes on How I Write

When I first saw Michelangelo's unfinished sculptures of *The Four Slaves* in the Accademia in Florence, I was struck by the figures, which had not quite emerged from the stone. Some seemed in a state of struggle that reminded me of how a story can remain unfinished for a long time, only half imagined. I knew that Michelangelo believed a block of marble already contained the figure within and that not till he saw it clearly could he begin to chisel away the extraneous material. In one of his sonnets he wrote: "The marble not yet carved can hold the form / Of every thought the greatest artist has."

Perhaps those figures of the slaves remained incomplete for some of the same reasons that stop a writer from going forward with her work. For me, the vision sometimes fades, the idea turns cold or uninteresting, or a more accessible and passionate idea takes my attention.

How I discover the form of a story (as well as the voice with which to tell it, the angle from which to view it) has always been a matter of timing. Sometimes I simply have to get older. Sometimes I discover that what I want to write isn't taking shape, so I'm forced to leave the body there, half on the page, half uncreated, still mired in a chunk of uncertainty. There is always the hope that someday I will return to the piece and, by working away at it, pushing through the block, see the real picture that hides in the general mass of emotion and action I'm trying to bring into focus.

Since childhood, I've felt compelled to write about the way things really are. At seven I wrote poems. Not long after, my father bought me a typewriter, which I took down to the basement of our Brooklyn house and set on a card table. I remember thinking to myself, "I'm alone now, and I'll write to someone who really understands." Someone, I meant, who was sensitive, compassionate, intelligent—all the things I was convinced my relatives and parents were not. I had an early conviction that I wanted to tell the whole truth about what I knew—and that this could not be done in argument or conversation with those in my family or in discourses to my dog. I could do this only by writing down and telling the truth on paper.

A few years later, my father, who was in the antique business, gave me a blank-paged printer's dummy of a book whose title was on the spine: *The Heritage of the Bounty*. The book had a gray cover (resembling in some ways the copy of *Gone with the Wind* we had in our house), and I seized upon it and recorded my thoughts in it daily. When I had just turned sixteen, I wrote this entry: "I feel I should do something in this life. Most of us leave the big things to others, less lazy than us. . . . I want to write something—to make people understand life better. First I must learn to understand it more myself."

All mixed up in my writing were "truths" and "fictions." Sometimes I could tell more of the truth if I invented a less murky setting for it, or cleared away people who didn't belong in the scene. Now and then I made some exaggerations to bring the truth into sharper relief. (In *Lives of the Artists*, Vasari writes that Michelangelo's method of extracting his four slaves from the stone was to "take a figure of wax, lay it in a vessel of water and gradually emerge it and then note the most salient parts. Just so, the highest parts were extracted first from the marble.")

When I created an effect, or emphasized "the highest parts," I had in mind the person, or god, or friend who might someday read my work and need my help to see clearly the essence of the story. Thus, as a child, committed to working out these truths and inventions, I set myself a lifelong job. Flannery O'Connor said that if you live to the age of five, you have enough to write about for the rest of your life. This was surely true for me.

Though *Gut Feelings* is a collection of essays, I chose to include three stories as "Minute Inventions." I have always felt these pieces wavered on the line between memoir and story because they seem to contain fewer "lies" than some of my others stories, although fictional lies are almost always a way of making the truth even truer. The use of the first person in all of them tends to confer an air of confession, a kind of intimacy, as do the titles of the stories (all of them quotations).

"This Is a Voice from Your Past" are the words a man whispers into the phone when he calls a woman who loved him years earlier in their college days. "I Don't Believe This" is what the young wife of a suicide tells her sister on the day he is to be cremated. "Tell Me Your Secret" is the name of a party game designed to seduce confessions and humiliations from its players. These stories emerged nearly full blown from remembered events so that (years after I wrote them) they now beg to be called memoir, rather than fiction.

I think it's a mistake to dismiss the work of many young fiction writers as "autobiographical" as if there were something self-evident and shameful about this—as if, when the writer is more mature, she'll give up this self-indulgence and get busy using her imagination. For me, there is no imagining without a basis in truth.

There were many "truths" in the story surrounding "I Don't Believe This." Years later, after I had some distance from, and an expanded understanding of, the same material, I wrote my novel *King of the World*, partly from the point of view of the tormented and mentally ill husband described in the story. Was this an act of "imagination" and thus a greater act of creativity? I think not. In creating this man, a person so far removed from myself in every sense, I had to examine more closely than ever the truths I knew. Though my male character was dangerous, deviant, and crazed, I thought I understood something deep about him. He was a man who had ideas he believed to be brilliant but that were rejected, who tried to do what he thought important and was not appreciated, who was refused and turned away time and again. I saw him not so much as an invention completely different from myself but as an extension of the writer in me who understood his state of mind. Writers, too, are often ignored and rejected, want approval and do not get it, have periods of deep disillusion and violent anger. Writers are dependent upon the judgment of others all their lives. Even when a writer has been working for thirty years, even if she has been sometimes successful, she still has to offer up any new piece she writes to the fads and tastes of the publishing world. I was able to write from this man's soul and know his disappointment, his frustration and his bafflement. As a writer I could be his voice.

∾

One of the memoirs in this collection, "The Treasures We Held," was submitted to the *Sewanee Review* as a piece of fiction. The *Review*'s editor, George Core, told me he would publish it in a forthcoming issue dedicated to the memoir form. At first I thought this was an unacceptable suggestion, but, after reading through the piece several times, I removed the fictional names and read it again. I could see that this narrative would work on either side of the line. Sometimes, a story (conceived as fiction but told in a straightforward way) appears to imitate memoir. Sometimes, a memoir, because it contains all the turns and twists that fiction must invent, seems to have been fictionally "altered." Now and then, a rare tale offers itself up with such wholeness that the writer feels it comes as a gift. This was the case with "The Lost Airman," the narrative about my cousin, the flier, who was shot down over New Guinea during World War II. The astonishing end of the story was revealed forty-five years after its beginning (the day of my cousin's disappearance, when I was not quite five years old). Then all I had to do was write it down.

"My Suicides," the stories of those I knew who had taken their own lives, was a more difficult piece to knit together. Two magazine editors wrote me almost identical rejection letters: "I don't see that you make any judgments in this piece on the nature of suicide." I was surprised that either of them believed it was the writer's job to judge or editorialize. The writer presents the picture and all that she can put into it. Judgment is left to the reader.

While most people live the experiences of their lives and move on, writers (maybe not all, but those whose base of material is autobiography) seem to have a compulsion to live at least twice. I learned the effects of this in the year after my father died suddenly, and very young, of leukemia. Until I wrote my first novel, *An Antique Man,* which is based on his death, I was unable to stop reliving in my mind every moment of his suffering and rapid decline. Once I captured this in its full dimensions on paper, I felt enormous relief that nothing of his ending would be forgotten, that all he endured (and we, his family, endured) was safe and available to me and no longer needed to run like an endless movie through my mind. Beyond that, I hoped I had made something more of it, a story for others to read.

I suppose the disadvantage of living twice (or more) to the usual once-per-real-event per person is that the time a writer spends writing about expired moments is not time free for looking forward and embracing the present. Still, if poetry is emotion recollected in tranquillity, then fiction (and memoir) are forms of emotion recollected in a state of even higher emotion. (I often laugh out loud or cry while writing.) Though it's a commonplace to say that writing is a lonely profession, the writer's desk is—at its best moments—the least lonely of workplaces.

My first novel was based on my father's life and death. I have since written four books in which my mother and her history, in various personas and guises, play a critical role. The first lines of the essay published here, "Getting Mother Buried" ("Twenty years before my mother was to die, she phoned me to say, 'I don't want any transients at my funeral'") appeared in a story of mine called "Witnesses," published fifteen years earlier. The approaching death of my mother's alter ego, Anna, was chronicled in two of my novels, *Anna in Chains* (1998) and *Anna in the Afterlife* (2002). In yet another guise, my mother's mortality is what ends my novel *The Kingdom of Brooklyn* (1992). My "real" mother is the subject of my nonfiction memoir *Old Mother, Little Cat: A Writer's Reflections on Her Kitten, Her Aged Mother . . . and Life* (1995).

No two of these books or stories have the same angle of vision or voice, though they treat, in some manner, the same powerful character. They are all written by me, but using numerous voices. I am sometimes myself as observer and sometimes myself in wolf's clothing; that is, I place myself in the narrator's mind and freely interpret and exaggerate what facts I know to be part the story. This freedom allows a blessed ventriloquism, gives license to express extremes of logic, politically incorrect prejudices, and fiercely bitter irony.

The stories of my life are the basis of my work, stories told more than once in new voices with different perspectives. My novel *Now Molly Knows* (1974) recounts in fictional form the events on which I based the essay "'Look How She Holds His Hand': A Memoir of Love in the 50s." Perhaps my need to use a few events in many ways is a function of living my days so dedicated to writing that wild and wrenching moments are scarce. Writing for hours each day is not a profession that encourages a lifestyle that's "a thrill a minute." Adventures do occur, it has been said, but not punctually. Still, since writing is my calling, I hope to be one "on whom nothing is lost." I wait to receive further news from existence and to give it due justice in the retelling.

Acknowledgments

Portions of this book were first published, some in a slightly different form, as follows:

"Follow the Thread into the Labyrinth: A Fond Recollection of Andrew Lytle," *The Chattahoochee Review*, fall 1988

"A Recollection of Wallace Stegner and the Stanford Writing Workshop," *The Sewanee Review*, winter 1995

"A Month in the Country at Yaddo," *The Sewanee Review*, fall 1996

"The Lost Airman," *Commentary Magazine*, June 1998

"The Treasures We Held," *The Sewanee Review*, fall 1995

"Getting Mother Buried," *The Chattahoochee Review*, fall 1998

"Look How She Holds His Hand," *The Sewanee Review*, winter 2002

"My Suicides," *Salmagundi*, winter 2002

"The Harpsichord on the Mountain," *The American Scholar*, summer 2002

"This Is a Voice from Your Past," *The Chattahoochee Review*, summer 1997, reprinted in *The Best American Mystery Stories*, 1998

"I Don't Believe This," *Atlantic Monthly*, 1984, reprinted in *Prize Stories: The O. Henry Awards*, 1986

"Tell Me Your Secret," *The Southwest Review*, January 2000

"A Few Words . . ." *Contemporary Authors Autobiography Series*, volume 20, Gale Research, Inc., 1994

Truths about Writing

Follow the Thread into the Labyrinth

A Fond Recollection of Andrew Lytle

When I first entered Andrew Lytle's writing class in 1957 (the year he published *The Velvet Horn*), I was a nineteen-year-old girl from Brooklyn who had come to the University of Florida by way of Miami Beach. My family had moved to Florida when I was fourteen to escape the cold winters of New York; to me "the south" was mainly a place where a person could get a good suntan.

Our writing class met at night in a rickety wooden structure. Mr. Lytle would arrive, smiling, his glasses strung around his neck on a black grosgrain ribbon, and greet us all heartily. The students sat around long wooden tables, and Mr. Lytle sat in a very old, over-stuffed chair. Behind him was a row of windows, and, beyond them, were the lights of the library, shining in at us. Beside Mr. Lytle, during each class, sat Smith Kirkpatrick, who also taught writing classes at the university and who was, even then, working on his novel *The Sun's Gold*. Kirk, with his kind, intense face, usually sat smoking, listening carefully. When Mr. Lytle could not elicit from us the answers he was seeking, he would finally turn to Kirk, who always knew the flaw or excellent thing to which Mr. Lytle was hoping to draw our attention.

Before discussing the students' stories, Mr. Lytle liked to read one of his own favorites to us. He was an inspired actor, and any story he read took on the dimension of theater. I can still see his face as he began reading Flannery O'Connor's "A Good Man Is Hard to Find." ("The grandmother didn't want to go to Florida. She wanted to visit some of her connections in east Tennessee and she was seizing at every chance to change Bailey's mind.") Mr. Lytle's eyes sparkled with the thrills he knew were coming. Now and then he could not contain himself and would burst out laughing as he read one perfect comic line after another.

On other nights he showed a more somber demeanor; when he read James Joyce's "The Dead" in class, Mr. Lytle became very serious, indeed. I still have the notes I took on the night of April 16, 1959 (I found them in the pages of our textbook, Gordon and Tate's *The House of Fiction*). Here are a few of the comments I took down that night:

> "Parts 1 and 2: Gabriel is in his last and sinning state. Part 3: Gabriel is regenerated."
> "The supernatural appears only through the natural."
> "The three fates (the three muses) are the three women—virgins—completed—living in death."
> "Debauchery and asceticism are both forms of death, one by denial, one by excessive use."
> "Age is dead youth."
> "The head is the upper phallus."
> "Trappist monks don't speak."
> "In the end we all come to earth." .

This kind of talk was heady stuff to a girl who, before college, had read widely in *Seventeen* magazine and who thought she aspired to publish there.

Each night when class ended, the women students had to race back to the dorms to get in by curfew. We were aware Mr. Lytle often stayed to talk with the men after class, but the women did not have such privileges. I knew that Mr. Lytle often visited the male students in their rooms and talked with them about life and art late into the night. The men in our class boasted of this—and I was jealous.

One day I took courage and asked to have a private conference with Mr. Lytle. I'd been writing a story about a young girl who was deeply troubled and who spent a long, hot summer crocheting a purple and yellow snake-like rope, which she wound into an ever-expanding rug. I called the story "The Purple and Yellow Summer," and I hadn't the slightest idea what it was about. It seemed sad enough and dense enough to be "artistic"; I thought he and I should talk about it. Mr. Lytle invited me to come to his study at his house in Gainesville. He told me he rose before dawn to work and asked that I arrive in the early morning, about eight. I distinctly remember walking to his house in the chill, woodsy morning. Fall leaves were underfoot, and the sun was newly up. I carried my "work" under my arm—never before had I felt so *serious;* I was a serious writer, on my way to have a talk with the great master.

Mr. Lytle showed me the carved wooden chair in his study; he pointed out the *ouroboros* on it; it was his favorite symbol—the snake eating its own tail. I indicated my story, which Mr. Lytle had already read, and asked him to help me with the characters and "the plot."

"What should I have them *do?*" I asked.

He thought for a moment. Then he said, "Merrill, there is only one way to write: you must follow the thread back into the labyrinth; there and only there you will find the meaning."

While I was pondering this (in fact, I am pondering it still), a call came from the house. Mrs. Lytle needed help! The baby had broken a jar of peanut butter, and all hands were needed in the cleanup!

I became acquainted with the family and made friends with the Lytles' two younger daughters, Kate and Langdon. On several occasions, I babysat for them. One evening, as the Lytles were getting ready to go out, Mr. Lytle's wife, Edna, came from her bedroom to give me some instructions about the children. She looked beautiful in a stunning red dress; when I admired it, she took me into her confidence. She smiled and said (rather mischievously), "When a woman turns forty, Merrill, she either takes a lover or buys a red dress."

꧁꧂

One afternoon I met Mr. Lytle on campus. "I trust you have a story to read in class tonight," he said. "I'm counting on you."

"Oh, yes, I have one," I said.

"Good, I'm looking forward to it." I watched him walk away, feeling extreme panic. It was 2:00 P.M. I had exactly five hours in which to invent and write a complete short story! I remember thinking, as I ran to my dormitory room, "He's *counting* on me!" I sat down and began to type. By 6:45 P.M., I had written a twelve-page story. When Mr. Lytle read it in class that night, no one knew the ink had barely dried on the paper. He admired the story publicly. He was proud of me.

Another time, I had written a story for class about a character I called "Crazy Harry"—Mr. Lytle was much taken with this story and told me that the following week, when he was leaving for New York to meet with his editor, he intended to bring the story himself, directly to the offices of the *New Yorker.* Imagine my state of mind during his absence! All week I waited for a telegram! None came. And, when I saw Mr. Lytle in class after his trip, he seemed to have no special news. In fact, he gave me no signal at all. After class, I tapped his arm, trembling.

"Mr. Lytle. What did the *New Yorker* say?"

"The *New Yorker?* Oh my! I forgot about that."

(That story, "The People in China," was later published in the *Florida Review.*)

It seems to me now that the students in our particular writing class (that year, that time, that place) constituted a sacred circle; we were blessed initiates in a mysterious and difficult art. Once the door to that small classroom was shut and Mr. Lytle began reading in his wonderful, expressive voice, a magical aura enclosed us. Many of us continued to write seriously: Mary Ann Taylor, Sue Richards (who married Dick Richards, also in our class), Frank Taylor, Charlie Rose, Tom Adams. Others—Ted Srygley, Jim Degnan, Jack De Bellis, Bill Glasser, Paul Hunter—stayed in touch for many years. Three from that group (Mary Ann Taylor and Sue and Dick Richards) lived in Sadieville, Kentucky, within farm's length of Andrew Lytle. For a number of years, all of them worked and lived as a small helping community.

In my first semester of graduate work, I applied for a small fellowship from the English department to help with expenses. I asked Mr. Lytle for a reference; he said he'd be happy to write one. To my delight, I was awarded the grant. When I went to collect my check, Alton C. Morris, then the head of the English department, seemed puzzled. He said, "Miss Gerber, on the strength of Mr. Lytle's extremely fine recommendation, we decided to give you this money, but now that I am looking at your transcript, I see that you aren't as brilliant as he said you are. Look at this—you had grades of C in the physical sciences!" With a look of extreme annoyance on his face, he handed me the envelope. "We hope we haven't made a mistake," he said.

∞

The following September, I came back to the University of Florida to begin a job as a graduate teaching assistant in the English department. A day before the semester formally began, I received a wire from Brandeis University informing me that a scholarship for which I had applied had just come through. I was beside myself with confusion. My husband-to-be was a graduate student at Brandeis; I wanted to be with him and to study literature in their graduate program. But I had committed myself to my rented room and promised my services to the university. (Also, I remembered Dr. Morris's comment.) I went to Andrew Lytle with my desperate dilemma; he suggested that I search my soul (that cloudy labyrinth?) and do what was necessary. When he saw the answer on my face, he led me to his green Cadillac, drove me to his bank, loaned me enough money to buy a plane ticket to Boston, rounded up some students to help me pack, and drive me to the airport. He kissed me goodbye and wished me Godspeed.

Wallace Stegner and
the Stanford Writing Workshop

It was late April in Boston, and I was in the ninth month of my first pregnancy. Three days before my baby was due to be born, I received a telegram from Wallace Stegner in California. He said that I had been chosen to receive a Stegner Fiction Fellowship and that he looked forward to seeing me at Stanford in the fall. He offered his congratulations to me!

Big as a battleship and on course for only one destination, I had completely forgotten that I'd applied for the fellowship. The news threw me into a turmoil; while my husband and I folded the newly washed virgin diapers (we had been advised to wash them no fewer than six times before use), we debated the wild possibility that we might accept my prize and go west. My husband had just been offered his first job, at Boston University, and I had forgotten, in the dizzying demands of the last weeks of pregnancy, that I was (or wanted to be) a writer.

We could not fail to see, however, that an opportunity was upon us; we knew it would never come again. We knew it would change our lives. We decided, in the vernacular of these times, to go for it.

Robert Stone and Ed McClanahan were Stegner Fellows with me that year (1962), and we met for the first time at a welcoming reception at Mary and Wallace Stegner's home. I had brought our infant daughter to the party and laid her on the Stegners' bed, surrounded by pillows. When I arrived in the living room, the first thing I saw was a large framed portrait of Wallace Stegner on the wall, and, an instant later, the man himself moved toward me through the crowd, *straight* toward me, looking directly at me. Tall, fair-haired, extraordinarily handsome, he extended his hand to me and greeted me with great warmth and kindness. I went slightly weak in the knees, realizing that I had really come to this place, that I had crossed the country, left family behind, come west with a two-month-old infant and barely any money but the $2,500 that I was to receive from the fellowship (and on which our small family would have to survive for the year). Yet, seeing his smile at that moment, I knew this day would mark our lives in some important way.

⁂

The fiction workshop became (together with my new baby) the center of my world. This was not my first encounter with a famous writing teacher in a respected writing program. As an undergraduate, I had studied at the University of Florida with Andrew Lytle, who at the time was finishing his celebrated novel *The Velvet Horn.* From the enormous energy Lytle had generated in our small writing class at Gainesville, I knew the potential that a writing workshop could unearth if it had the proper chemistry; I knew what it was like to be galvanized into action, to feel the pressure of my own talent (especially when acknowledged by others), and to find the focus and means to express it. Lytle's class had been an extraordinary awakening for me, and he an exceptional supporter. Although there was a clear demarcation between the master and his students, he also made personal contact with those of us he felt "had the calling," engendering in us a powerful sense of responsibility toward our gift and toward him. I had every hope that the Stegner workshop would also stir my energies in new and wondrous ways.

We met once a week on the Stanford campus, in the Jones Room of the main library, along with other members of the advanced writing class. Seated around a large oval table, we offered up for criticism the efforts we'd worked on all week. What motivated us as we sat at home trying to write was the knowledge that the others were at their typewriters typing away and that Wally Stegner would be listening to our words and sometimes reading them aloud so that we could listen to our own rhythms.

Though Stegner could perceive in an instant the flaws in a piece of fiction (the weak link, the parts we'd hurried over, the emotions we didn't understand and tried to sail past, the sloppy construction of a sentence or the misfit of even one word), he preferred to keep silent at first, to remain in the background and allow the class to thrash out their differences. Only when he observed that we were not even close, had missed the fatal flaw, did he step forward and offer his advice.

The first story I wrote in his workshop was about a young woman who gives birth to a daughter and whose mother comes to stay with her in order to help out. The experience turns out to be a nightmare. I felt safe writing this story (a revelation of intimate family dynamics, as well as an expose of some dangerously raw hostilities) three thousand miles from my mother, nowhere near the scene of the crime, among supportive strangers. Wally Stegner made it clear that in his workshop we were free of constraints of conscience (not of literary conscience!) and free of the forms that protected us in ordinary society. Good artistic taste was the measure, not "good" taste. Here, in the workshop, we could let it all out, say it the way we saw it, take great risks, as long as we said it well, said it honestly, said it powerfully. And *never* (he stressed) were we to assume that the narrator or protagonist was one and the same as the author. At least we had that much protection.

Stegner seemed to have an aversion to following (or having us follow) any theoretical or philosophical principles relating to the writing of fiction. He often said, "I don't know what I think till I see what I say." He wanted us to sit down and *write*—and only afterward to turn on our "editing" mind, see what we'd produced, and go about shaping it, ordering it, and refining it.

⌦

The story I wrote in Stegner's workshop about the mother and daughter (which was, of course, "fiction"), I called "A Daughter of My Own"; it was received in class with enormous enthusiasm and very few criticisms. I remember Wally standing at the side of the room, smiling enigmatically, as if he had known all along that I was going to pull it off. Buoyed by my success among my peers, I asked whether the story was ready to send off into the great maw of the literary marketplace. We discussed "markets" at that time (Wally knew a fair amount about the "selling" end of the writing business and was willing to share information with us, whereas Andrew Lytle, as I recall, felt it unseemly to discuss the commercial aspects of writing when "art" should be our primary concern).

I decided to send my story off to *Redbook* magazine, and within days I heard from the editors that they wanted to buy it! This was triumph, indeed—to be able to walk into class and to report to those who had been present at its birth, so to speak, that the creature was not only viable but salable! (It did not occur to me till much later that eight million copies of it would find their way into drugstores and doctors' waiting rooms and that my mother would be certain to see it!) Wally was suitably proud of my sale, but cautious. Caution was his byword: don't get too puffed up, don't get too confident, don't get too sure of yourself. The next story will be just as hard to write, maybe harder. It probably won't sell. You can't keep your eye on the marketplace; you have to keep it on the work. The rest comes, or it doesn't come—but that's not the focus.

Chastened, and fortified for the blow certain to come, I wrote my second story, "We Know that Your Hearts Are Heavy," about the funeral of an uncle. I sent it to the *New Yorker,* which bought it. By return mail. Those in the workshop looked at me with some suspicion, I felt. But, no, I had no agent, I had no connections, I had no reputation. My ship had merely come in. This was easy! All I had to do from now on was type for a few hours a day, and someone would publish what I wrote. I was jubilant. Wally Stegner did not caution me again, but he made it clear that I should restrain myself. He knew the ways of the world. He knew this was like the passing of a comet—it happened only every century or so.

But I was not the only Fellow for whom the comet appeared. That year, Houghton Mifflin awarded Bob Stone its literary fellowship. Because he had no phone, one of the company's editors called me. She entrusted me with the news and asked me to get it to Bob.

My husband and I hurried over to his little rented house, and I fairly banged the door down with excitement. When I told him about his award, we danced around together on the rickety wooden porch in jubilation.

⸎

I did my writing in our little Stanford Village two-room apartment (in what used to be an army barracks), on a manual typewriter supported on a plank laid across two tall wooden crates. My husband, who was homebound and baby-sitting, had decided to build a harpsichord out of a kit. (He deserves special acknowledgment, I think, since this was not yet the era of househusbands and liberated wives.) While I was writing my stories, he kept the baby's supplemental bottle warming on one burner of the stove and melted lead in a tin pot on the other in order to weight the keys on the harpsichord.

We bought an old car and found that we could get free clothes for the baby at the "Trading Post," a used clothing exchange near the laundry machines in the center of Stanford Village. We liked living in the converted barracks among other married students, many of whom had babies who became acquainted with our daughter. (I tried to forgive the university for denying us campus housing when we first arrived; the secretary in the housing office had claimed that it was the rule to give only married *male* students with families apartments in Stanford Village, but, after she saw the infant in my arms, and after I said I intended to write an angry letter to the president of the university (for what other power did I have but that in my pen?), she reconsidered, made some phone calls, and allowed that she could stretch the rules and give us space. The rent was $52 a month, including utilities. On that scale, we could just about make ends meet.

⸎

We often gathered at the Stegners' home, which was in a wooded and secluded area of Los Altos Hills. Theirs had been the only house on their road until recently. The Stegners seemed troubled as others gradually built on neighboring hillsides and crowded the landscape with buildings and visible wires. From their patio, they pointed out to us the growing scars on the landscape.

Illustrious visitors sometimes dropped in. Malcolm Cowley was there one evening, and, distracted from his discourse on literature, he got down on the floor to play with my baby daughter, delighting in her resemblance to his own grandchild. Wally was relaxed with us, always cordial and kind. The parties at the Stegners' house were of the classic sort: wonderful food, serious conversation, the sharing of good literature, good music. But I felt his pulling back from what was happening, in a general sense, on campus. The sixties were taking hold in a big way. We knew of other types of parties going on around Palo Alto. Drugs were bursting onto the scene. I had heard the stories about Ken Kesey but hadn't met him yet. There were rumors of amazing and wild goings-on in the vicinity of a street known as Perry Lane. Wally seemed a little uncomfortable with the turn the world was taking. As a man who respected the earth and its natural glories, he also respected and cherished the workings of his mind—he wanted nothing to do with turning on and tuning out. He clearly wished to be present in his unaltered consciousness at all times, to witness the process that went on within, to observe the scenes that took place without, especially in the natural world.

My husband and I let the psychedelic world spin on its merry way, finding our own world colorful enough, with the new baby to keep us delighted and entertained, with my stories falling onto the page in rapid and splendid prose (or so I thought), and with his harpsichord taking shape, slowly, in a corner of the living room, its angular walnut sides gleaming with wood wax, its strings being strung, its plectra being cut and fine-tuned with an X-acto knife.

Even though I was the only female Fellow, I made myself available to talk shop with the male Fellows at our various social gatherings, but, inevitably, given the nature of that era, I would find myself out of the circle and would drift away to talk with the wives of the men; Bob Stone's wife, Janice, had a little girl, and Ed McClanahan's wife, Kit, also had a daughter, and both women (a year or two ahead of me in the raising of children) had much advice for me. The men had other concerns; Bob was writing what was to become his novel *A Hall of Mirrors,* and Ed was in the process of working on his book about a fatal schoolbus accident. I was still heady with the success of my two sales, and it seemed the world was getting rosier every day.

One morning we heard a bulletin on the radio that the United States government had detected Russian missiles in Cuba. Furthermore, many reserve units (and they named them, including my husband's Air Force Reserve Unit) were being called into service.

War! How could such a threat come into our cozy den, where literature and music and stuffed teddy bears were the gods, and where our golden-haired little daughter had begun to show signs of awareness, language, humor? Within a matter of days, my husband was packed and gone away to Hamilton Air Force Base, north of San Francisco, and I was left alone, with a car I couldn't drive, with a little baby for whom I was solely responsible, and with my typewriter on a plank for company and consolation.

Everyone in the writing program heard the news and knew of my plight. Kit and Janice offered to baby-sit for me on the days of the workshop, Mary Stegner called and offered her help, Wally took it in stride. Writers had to face these matters head on, and with a stoic attitude. Even if my husband were called away to war in Cuba, I'd manage somehow. I had the goods to cope. I had a good mind. I was here at Stanford as proof of that, wasn't I? Negotiating these roadblocks was one of the challenges of life.

Wally's message fortified me, reminded me to try to study every aspect of each experience, to try to make sense of it. I wrote another story, and another. Nothing seemed to lessen my energy for writing that year. My husband, still not knowing whether he'd be sent to Cuba, was able to come home on weekends and to take away with him parts of the harpsichord to work on at the base. (He was trained in the operation of the teletype, but not much was going on in teletype operations at the time.)

One day I came home from class to find in the mail a letter from a major Boston publisher. It contained an offer for my first book of stories! The terms made me heady with joy—the company would give me an advance of $150, on the condition that, after my book was completed and in the editors' hands, if they didn't like it, they could reject it, and I would return to them half of the advance.

Given my recent successes, I had no doubt that they would like it and publish it. I could almost feel the book in my hands. I called Wallace Stegner and told him I had to see him, at once, at once. I was levitating. Gravity seemed to have no effect on me. Wally said he would meet me at the library within the hour. I don't remember how I got to campus—I may have flown on my own wings.

Wally greeted me with his wise, patient smile. I always responded to his presence by feeling a burst of inner confidence, and I think the other Fellows did, too. Because his standards were so high, for himself and for us, we seemed to be able to call up our deepest resources to satisfy his expectations. I felt certain the news I was flying to tell him would delight him, and I was pleased to demonstrate to him that he had not made a mistake in his judgment by choosing me for the fellowship.

I held out the letter from the publisher. He read it once, twice. He examined it seriously. He rubbed his chin. He looked at the second page of the letter, which was a miniature contract. If I signed on the solid line, we had a deal.

"You just tell them you're sorry," Wally said to me. "You appreciate their interest, but you have other irons in the fire."

"But I don't!" I cried.

"But you will," he said.

"But aren't they a big publishing house? Aren't they respectable?"

"Their offer isn't respectable," Wally said. "They want you to give them *half* back if they don't like the book? Half of $150?"

"Oh," I said. "I guess that isn't very good, then."

"You hold out for what you're worth," Wally instructed me. And in his eyes I could see my worth blooming, like a flower taking on color and beauty.

Before the year was out, I had an offer from another Boston publisher for nearly fifteen times the amount of the first offer—with *no* conditions and no suggestion that the company "might not like it."

⌘

Wally and I corresponded for thirty years after those fine days, and, when my middle daughter was a student at Stanford, we visited him and Mary at their home. We laughed about my streak of astounding good luck in the early weeks of my fellowship, and I certified that my pile of rejections would now be able to give any writer a run for his money.

Last October, when I sent Wally a copy of my fifth novel, *The Kingdom of Brooklyn,* he wrote these words to me: "You've done it this time. . . . You've worked very long and hard, and you're a finished artist now. And I don't mean 'done with.' Mary and I both read the book with fascination. So will many others, the more the merrier. We're very happy about this one."

A Month in the Country at Yaddo

There is no rule against looking for inspiration, but Yaddo cannot guarantee that anyone will find it.

                    Booklet sent by Yaddo to prospective Fellows

Fifteen years ago, when the taxi let me off at the entrance to the Yaddo Mansion in Saratoga Springs, New York, I was met by a young man who introduced himself as Allan Gurganus. He said that, because he had been a guest at Yaddo many times, he sometimes had the privilege of showing new visitors to their quarters. He picked up my suitcase and invited me to follow him to my room. Though I had sent ahead, from California, a trunk full of letters and notes for the novel I was writing (as well as my portable typewriter), these items had not yet arrived. I told the young man I hoped my trunk wasn't lost—that I couldn't write a word without it since it contained "all my raw material."

He said, "Everyone comes here with tons of raw material. It's what you do with it that counts."

Somewhat chastened, I followed behind him as he climbed up a back staircase, then up a second flight of stairs and down a long hallway. The higher we got, the hotter it got. The room whose door he opened was an attic room with a slanted ceiling. Large steam pipes hung overhead from metal brackets; the afternoon heat was so intense in the small space that I set my shoulder bag down on the bed and sat suddenly on a hard wooden chair. At that moment, I noticed a pile of silver chains folded on the floor in front of the window.

"In case of fire," Allan said, "you throw that ladder over the windowsill and climb out. If you need anything else, you can let me know at dinner time. You'll have a studio in the woods as well, so when your other things arrive, we'll get you settled there."

I thanked him—then asked him if anyone important had ever stayed in my room.

"We don't talk about things like that here," he said, with a kindly tone of reprimand. "Everyone is equally important."

I stopped asking questions. When he saw me wipe my brow with my handkerchief, he said, "Maybe we can try to get you a fan. I'll see if there's one not spoken for." As he closed the door behind him, I understood for a fact that no one important had ever stayed in *this* room.

⬖

After resting for a while and then hanging a few shirts in the closet, I ventured into the hallway. The first door I came to had a typed card thumbtacked on it: "This door is never to be opened, for any reason, ever."

Further down the corridor, I found a bathroom with the door ajar. The fixtures were ancient, and there was no lock on the door. Water resting in the toilet bowl was rust-brown in color, as was the water that came out of the tap in the sink.

I returned to my room and lay down on the narrow, high bed. I contemplated my situation. I wondered why I had come so far from my home and its comforts, from my husband and my three daughters. I wondered whether I had the courage to do what had to be done. I remembered having told myself many times (this attraction was, in a way, my primary reason for coming to Yaddo) that for an entire month I would be served (instead of serving) three meals a day. This benefit now seemed faint recompense for all the losses I suddenly counted.

⬖

Just as I came into the Grand Hall where the guests had gathered before dinner, I heard a cry: "Watch out, it's a bat!" A number of women screamed and covered their heads, while the men began rushing about shouting instructions to one another. One man appeared with a net attached to an incredibly tall pole. I stood and watched while the pandemonium swirled around me. After a while—when no bat was captured or even glimpsed—the wild buzz modulated and conversation began again, muted by the hanging tapestries, the velvet drapes, and the brocade chairs. At the far end of the hall were the stained glass windows prized by Katrina and Spencer Trask, who (after the deaths of their four children) made Yaddo into a retreat for artists.

Having no one to talk to, I wandered around the enormous room, looking at the carved sleigh chair, the ornate wooden eagle on a mahogany stand, the marble busts, the rare antiques, the oil paintings. A wide red-carpeted staircase led to a reading area above, where I found, when I climbed up the steps, current issues of literary quarterlies, journals, and magazines. Located throughout the mansion, I knew, were the rooms of other artists—not one room, I was sure, furnished as mine was.

When the dinner gong sounded, I followed the others into the dining room and found an empty place at a table. I asked a woman, sitting in the chair next to the one I stood behind, if I might sit there. She looked at me quizzically as if wondering what I might be doing there, then announced that the seat was saved for a friend.

I backed away and walked around the room till I saw, at a large table near the far end of the dining hall, a young black woman sitting with an older black man. They watched me approach.

"Do you mind if I sit here with you?" I asked. "Are you saving these places for anyone?"

"Do be our guest," said the woman, with a rather grand gesture. "Though you can tell: this isn't the Captain's Table." She laughed, inviting me to laugh with her. Then the three of us introduced ourselves to one another. These two kind human beings were the painter Michael Kendall, and the writer John O. Killens. Both are now dead—John died in 1987, and Michael in July 1995 at the age of forty-two, of breast cancer.

⟡

In time, I learned the rules of the institution: between breakfast and 4:00 P.M. no guest must disturb another. After breakfast, each artist must pick up his black metal lunch pail (reminiscent of the kind that coal miners carry down to the mines) and lunch alone in his room or studio; after 4:00 P.M. the pails must be returned to be cleaned and refilled for the next day's lunch. It was understood that no guest would ever be summoned from his room for a phone call. There was one public phone in the mansion near the dining hall; friends and family must be directed to make calls only at dinnertime, when guests would be nearby to take them.

At 4:00 P.M., when the curfew lifted, guests were welcome to go into town in the car driven by the handyman who provided this service—to pick up snacks or cigarettes or bottled drinks (running water in the mansion was undrinkable). There would be stops at the post office, the bank, the stationery store.

As it happened, on the day my trunk arrived (intact, with all raw material in perfect shape), it turned out that my typewriter was hopelessly broken. At 4:00 P.M., I went into town in the Yaddo station wagon to buy the only typewriter left in the stationery store, a portable electric. I paid an unspeakably exorbitant price, came back with it, and set it up on a rickety table in my attic room. All around the mansion—all day and sometimes into the evening—I could hear typewriters clacking. The urgency of the keystrokes, coming from all directions, made me feel as if a race had begun and I was late to the starting gate. Perhaps this had something to do with the fanfare we heard daily from the Saratoga Race Course, located just at the edge of Yaddo's four-hundred-acre estate. After the fanfare, I thought, or imagined, I could hear the horses hooves pounding on the turf. "Hurry," I told myself, "write your book, your masterpiece—this is your chance. Do it now, or all will be lost."

❧

Allan, who had welcomed me the first day of my arrival, led me to my studio in the woods. I carried my new typewriter in its brown plastic case. We walked past the Yaddo library, past West House and Pine Garde, two smaller houses where guests also lived and worked, and past various other landmarks, the vegetable garden, the artists' studios, the towers where the composers wrote music—we also passed, at some point, one or two of the four lakes on the property. The geography of the place never became clear to me; I was forever lost, trying to locate the mansion or the pool or the tennis court with no North Star to fix on. Clearly though, my studio was miles away from the mansion. It seemed to me that my typewriter weighed fifty pounds by the time we got into the woods, where Allan directed my attention to a small wooden cabin, deeply hidden in the trees.

I stepped up on the hollow-sounding floorboards and looked inside. I saw a dark room containing a wooden desk and desk chair. I saw a metal cot with a very thin cotton mattress upon it. Dead flies were piled on the windowsills. I slapped at a mosquito buzzing around my ear.

"Isn't there . . . any running water?" I asked. I was looking for a bathroom.

He told me that most of the artists took bottled water to their studios. As well as the thermos that came with lunch.

"Where is your studio?" I asked.

Allan told me that he wrote in his room at the mansion. His room was big and very comfortable, with a view of the lawn and rose garden. Not everyone, he suggested, was lucky enough to be assigned a studio in the woods. I set my new typewriter down on the desk and, thinking of its cost, looked to see whether there was a lock on the door. I realized that nothing was locked at Yaddo. Even entry to the mansion, with all its precious antiques, was available to everyone. A key hung on a nail just to the side of each of its entrances.

As Allan wished me a productive afternoon of work and stepped out the door, I understood that, if I let him go, I'd have to find my own way back to the mansion. Furthermore, if I wanted to work at night, I'd have to come to my studio after dinner every evening, through the woods. And *then* I'd have to walk back to my room, alone, late at night, through these same dark and ominous paths, with heaven knew what kind of wild animals lying in wait for me. Still, there could be magic here. I thought of the list of the illustrious who had written their words at this place, perhaps even in this cabin—Eudora Welty, Saul Bellow, John Cheever, Malcolm Cowley, Wallace Stegner, Bernard Malamud, Katherine Anne Porter, Philip Roth, Sylvia Plath, Carson McCullers. The faces of the great—these and many others—spun around the room. But still, those woods at night. No, not for me, a city girl! Not for me, this Spartan cabin, lacking a toilet, lacking a phone, lacking . . .

I killed a mosquito on my arm and wiped the blood away with the side of my hand. Then I packed up my new typewriter and told Allan I simply would prefer—for the time being—to write in my attic room. I'd forgo the romance of writing in the woods even if Shakespeare himself might have composed at that old, scarred desk.

⌘

Curtis Harnack, the director of Yaddo at that time, and his wife, Hortense Calisher, lived in the one truly modern building on the property. I had spoken to Hortense only once, briefly, as she swept dramatically through the Grand Hall one night in a floor-length gown. Knowing that one of her books had been published by my then publisher, I suggested to her that sometime, perhaps, we might have a talk about him. "Not now, of course," I added, indicating that we could pursue this at a more appropriate time.

Her answer was: "Not now and not *ever*. That's New York talk— we don't talk about things like that here!"

I could see the house she and Curtis lived in from the pool, where residents were allowed to sun and swim . . . but where it was not advisable to talk. The few times I approached the pool, carrying my lunch pail and my notebook, I saw guests seated far apart, wearing sunglasses, each one reading or scribbling in deep concentration. I had already learned the dangers of talking to guests without invitation. One morning, while taking an early walk, I had made the mistake of greeting an artist on the path as she came toward me. "Good morning," I'd said. She replied fiercely as she hurried past me, head down, "I don't talk in the mornings!"

Therefore, at the pool, I knew better than to ask anyone, "How's the water today?" I took a chair and pulled it as far from another human being as was possible; the only sounds were of the wind in the trees, the gasps of a swimmer gulping air as he did laps in the pool, and the rustle of notebook pages as writers flipped them back to reread what they had written.

⌘

As for myself, I couldn't seem to write a word. My trunk, which contained material for my long-planned family-saga novel, seemed an alien thing, distasteful. Inside were the letters of the dead airman, my cousin, who had been shot down by Japanese Zeros in World War II, as well as letters to me from his mother, detailing our family's history in America from the time of my grandmother's flight from Poland to these shores in 1890. I had much more compelling things to think about, it seemed to me. I had seen The Greek-God Poet and The Spanish Princess jogging in the woods together; hours later they came back, she wearing a tiger-lily in her hair. And I had seen the Sculptress of Metallic Leaves go into the studio of the Artist Who Painted Burning Buildings. Some of these romances, I knew, were developing among unmarried guests, but others, I gathered, were not so unmarried. I had many new thoughts and sensations in myself to examine, and nothing at all seemed compelling or even vaguely interesting about my "raw material."

One evening during dinner, Curt Harnack came to sit briefly with Michael, John, and me at what we now called among ourselves "The Outcasts' Table." He asked how I was doing, and I confessed that I was unable to work at all. Maybe because my room was too hot. Maybe because my chair was rickety. Maybe . . .

He consoled me by saying that many writers were unable to work during their first stay at Yaddo and compared it to arriving at a new high school. The issues of figuring out where you stood in the pecking order, who would be your friends, and how the system worked were very distracting. He assured me I'd do better the next time I came as a guest to Yaddo. He confided that his role as director included being part mental-health counselor and part referee: "You have all these egos here, all this naked need, all this childlike genius—you're bound to have conflicts."

The next morning, Curt stopped me in the Grand Hall: a guest had left unexpectedly the night before and there was a vacancy in Pine Garde, one of the smaller residence houses. He said that this room, unlike all the others, actually had an air conditioner in it. Would I like to move? He understood that my room (which I now thought of as being in the servants' quarters of the house) was very hot, and he knew my accommodations could bear improving.

Without hesitation, I accepted his offer. Within a half hour I had gone upstairs and packed up all my goods and was waiting for the handyman to arrive to help me move. This young man was an extremely genial, handsome, and helpful person who drove the station wagon into town, picked up the mail for the residents, and—Michael and I had conjectured—incited fantasies in the dreams of many of the young poetesses and maybe in those not so young. I myself had watched him check for a leak in my clothes closet (he had to remove a handful of my underwear from a shelf to be able to inspect the wall), and I had a flash of Lady Chatterley and Mellors, the gamekeeper. Literary fantasies—and other sorts, as well—seemed easily accessible to me in my present state of loneliness and need.

My new room had a large double bed, a view of a majestic pine tree directly in front of my window, and the blessed cool breath of the air conditioner. I set my typewriter on a handsome, large desk and wondered why the guest who had occupied this room had left so suddenly. Inventing rumors was a favorite pastime at Yaddo; the imaginative powers of the guests were formidable. One story going the rounds had it that a female guest who shared a bathroom with a male guest had discovered on the sink, one day, a bottle of medicine for killing body lice. She went to the director and insisted that the person be asked to leave the premises. How he worked this out, if the tale was true, I will never know. But guests did leave very suddenly, we all knew, without explanation.

We had heard that a famous poet who arrived one night was terrified by ghosts. Apparently he took seriously the stories about the spirits that haunted Yaddo. Of the Trasks' four children, two had died of diphtheria, and two had drowned in terrible accidents in the lakes. Their ghosts were said to roam the gardens and buildings at night. On the night the poet arrived (so the story went), he saw the faces of the dead children looking into his second-story window. He piled his books and suitcases back into his car and sped away.

Michael and I talked a good deal about ghosts. Unlike me, she was not so doubting. She'd seen a few in her day, though she was only twenty-seven when we met. (She had already made history as the first black artist, and the youngest ever, to participate in the NASA Art Project. She had been honored with a commission from the United States government to do a painting of the space shuttle

Columbia.) One moonless night, Michael told me, she had been coming back through the woods from her studio to West House, where she lived, when she heard a strange clicking noise behind her. When she stopped walking, the noise stopped. When she sped up, it started up again. When she ran, it rushed, loud and fearsome, right behind her. Finally she took courage and looked back. And there she saw her Walkman radio, dragging and clanking along on the ground behind her!

On another night, when many of the guests had gone into town together (and again, since we had not grown more popular with the in-crowd, had left us out of the party), Michael asked me if I'd like to see the vacated music studio in the attic floor of West House. It was quite a luxurious place, she said, with two pianos, a soft rug, many couches and chairs. It would be a good place for us to talk.

We went upstairs and sat down to a long evening of shared confidences—complaints about Yaddo (though we agreed on our appreciation of the wonderful food), longings for our home places, and a diatribe against the mosquitoes. I showed her pictures of my husband and three daughters, and she told me of her cousin named Rocko who had come back from the dead to give her mother a message. Just as she was describing a visit from this ghost, Michael jumped, startled, and quickly pulled up the leg of her blue jeans. There we both saw a line of ants that had somehow managed to creep up her leg. She stamped her foot hard to shake them off. Then she stamped it again, twice. With the ants thus vanquished, we resumed our quiet conversation, but suddenly we heard a pounding of footsteps on the stairs leading to the attic. All at once, the door flew open, and a man and two women—guests who lived in West House—leaped into the room, brandishing brooms and pot covers. They began a wild dance, screaming and banging the brooms and pot covers. Michael and I jumped up and grabbed each other. Then the posse recognized who we were. They collapsed against each other, laughing. "My God," they explained, all talking at once. "We heard knocks from up here. Three distinct knocks! And we knew no one was living here now. We thought we heard ghosts!"

⊂∞⊃

On the fourth of July, a party was organized to drive to a nearby lake to see fireworks. As a Yaddo group event, even the "non-insiders" were invited to come along. We were asked to meet in the Grand Hall just after dinner. Because it was an extremely hot and humid night, most of the guests convened unburdened by baggage of any sort and wearing only shorts and thin cotton shirts. Except for two of us: myself and a young woman artist named Lorraine Shemesh. Unlike the others, she and I each carried an umbrella, a sweater, and a carry-bag (mine contained a bottle of water and a high-energy snack).

Lorraine came over to me: "Don't tell me," she said. "You have a Jewish mother, too!" We recognized at once that we were kindred spirits (and we are close friends to this day). Lorraine, that summer, was working, in her inimitable style, on a large drawing, in pencil, of a shoe bag. In it were shoes representing the entire full-spectrum life of a modern young woman: low-heeled pumps, fuzzy bunny slippers, Nike running shoes, summer sandals, and a pair of sexy spiked heels. I loved her work, humane and humorous and full of love as it was, and, one day, after I had told her that I was a secret belly-dancer, she made a gift for me from pastel chalks and a cardboard cutout: a belly-dancer on a stick. I treasure it still: a sexy lady in a blue bikini top and gauzy pants carrying, above her head, on a platter, a cooked chicken. She saw in my spirit the primary faces of womankind: seductress . . . and housewife.

Like high school friends unable to reach each other on the phone to discuss vital matters, we began to meet secretly, during the forbidden hours of the day, to get to know each other. Coming surreptitiously to her studio, I showed her the story I was (finally!) working on, not about the Lower East Side at the turn of the century but about Brooklyn this very summer, a story concerning a young boy I had loved when I was eleven years old and had only just spoken to for the first time in thirty-two years when I was passing through New York on my way to Yaddo. (The story, "Good-bye, Arny Goldstone," was published in *Redbook* and later included in the collection of my stories *This Old Heart of Mine,* published by Longstreet Press in 1993.)

So now—at last—I had a friend or two. Michael and John invited me one evening to accompany them to a night spot in Saratoga

Springs, a jazz and blues cafe, located upstairs over some stores. Lena, the woman who ran it, was famous for her musical guests and for her own guitar playing. In the laid-back atmosphere of the place, I suddenly felt that the summer was coming into focus and was not going to be so bad after all.

⌒∞⌒

The reason I finally was able to work at this point (I was already well on my way into a second story) seems to have had something to do with my meeting Gail Godwin in the Grand Hall one night, with having a cool and secure (and even attractive) place in which to write, and with having overcome my resistance to the unnatural state of enforced silence and isolation required by Yaddo's rules.

I recognized Gail Godwin by the back of her head, from her beautiful and thick wavy hair, which I'd seen in her book jacket photographs. I approached her tremulously, still feeling myself diminished and made insecure, somehow, by every small disappointment and insult I'd sustained here. (I never did understand how I came to be given my room in the attic: was it the only room left when my name came up for assignment? Was I so insignificant, and so unknown—even invited by *accident?*—that I was offered a space hardly better than a closet? In any case, my new quarters had instilled in me an improved sense of entitlement.) I introduced myself to Gail by saying that I had read and admired her novels. She turned to me graciously, saying that she was just visiting for the evening, that she loved Yaddo and in fact had met the man she lived with here. She asked my name, and, when I told it to her, she told me she knew of *my* work and had read it with admiration and delight. Though my encounter with her involved no more than that brief exchange, it served to remind me of my own accomplishments, and also of my mission.

Finally, though, I had convinced myself that my "old" way of writing, which meant finding rare chinks of time in the busy life I led raising three girls (all born within five years' time), was not the only way I could force myself to concentrate. I had become a mother at the age of twenty-four (and had moved to California immediately thereafter with my husband and first child—who was then only two months old—to accept a Wallace Stegner Fiction Fellowship at Stanford). My lifelong pattern of work involved writing while my babies were playing at my feet, or while dinner was cooking on the stove, or while the noise of family life swirled around my ears.

These defined hours of total silence at Yaddo unnerved me, whereas I could tell from the gratitude of many of the other guests that this span of time, disconnected from reality, was a blessing for them. I knew, also, that many of them were repeat visitors who had long ago come to terms with the elitism of those from the old guard, the most famous, and those who considered themselves above it all. During my summer visit, there were thirty or more guests present, and not all of them were dancing the nights away or having trysts behind the potting shed.

In any case, I was grateful to be able to settle down, even if uneasily, and get some work done.

∽◈∾

When I think of some of the other guests with whom I shared my life that summer, I give them special names. The Must-Quit-Smoking Journalist (she carried Tootsie Pops with her or urged others to buy her candy bars to satisfy her craving during this ordeal), the Dowager (a revered critic and writer who especially disliked being disturbed—everything was an interruption to her creative trance), the Bug-Spray Musician (each day, when he went to his studio in the woods, he sprayed his entire body with the insect repellent OFF), the Love-Sick Poetess (she monopolized the phone during the dinner hour every night, communing with her lover in New York), the Tree Artist (she painted only white spruce trees and nothing else). A group of gay men often went out together in the evenings—and left in my mind an image of bright-colored shirts, white silk vests, and gold-tipped canes.

One afternoon, after three weeks away from home, I saw a young child walking in the rose garden with his parents, and I longed desperately to see my own family. I realized I had not seen a child, or a pet, or my own bed in so long that I contemplated leaving Yaddo and taking the next plane back to California. My mood must have been evident, because, after breakfast the next day, the musician

David Del Tredici took me aside for a little pep talk. He told me that Yaddo affected everyone this way at one time or another; we were in a strange dimension here, cut off from the real world, up at the wire to test whether our talent was real or imaginary. He urged me to take heart. He made me promise to stay out my term. He went back to his room and returned carrying an apple and a pear for me—gifts to comfort me. Whenever I hear his beautiful "Alice" compositions, I remember with gratitude his effort to restore my energies.

⁓⊗⁓

The month of my arrival was also the wedding month of Prince Charles and Princess Diana. One of the guests that summer was a woman who wrote celebrity articles for popular magazines, and under no circumstances did she wish to miss that famous wedding. Televisions, however, were forbidden at Yaddo. Much plotting and whispering went on in the Grand Hall before dinner one night. It seemed that one of the New York artists had brought a TV up to Yaddo in his car and was planning to smuggle it into his studio for the event. An underground party was planned, complete with potato chips and M&Ms and a generous complement of liquor. But invitations went out only to a selected few.

I think that many of the artists at Yaddo were like children that summer. Relieved of heavy responsibilities in the complex lives they'd left behind and without a single pressing urgency to jog them into reality (no one ever had to write a check, pay a bill, shop at the grocery store), they sometimes resorted to children's games, children's cruelty, and to the dangerous plotting and mocking that take delight in excluding those who are not in the sacred circle. Although by the end of my stay I had made some important friendships, I was always aware of the cliques that opened and closed in a constant dance of you-come-in, you-keep-out.

⁓⊗⁓

Toward the end of my month at Yaddo, I was looking for the room of the Must-Quit-Smoking Journalist (she was in need of some soap powder for the washing machine, and I had offered to give her what was left of mine) when I took a wrong turn somewhere in the mansion and was soon totally lost. I climbed up one staircase, down another, up yet another, looking for a familiar landmark, when, suddenly, I found myself following a banister of coiled gold braid that ended at the room of a young novelist. She was writing at her desk and looked up in surprise when she found me at her open door. Inviting me in, she told me this had been Katrina Trask's bedroom. I could see it was the most magnificent of all rooms in the mansion, situated on the top floor, with a wide-window view of the great lawn and the gardens and of the trees and mountains beyond. The young woman showed me Katrina's white canopy bed, her matching desk with throne chair, and the private door to what seemed to be the slanted roof outside. When I asked to where the door led, she urged me to step outside and look—but to be careful.

I found myself miles above the earth, with a heavenly vista before me. There, nailed to the granite wall, was a bronze plaque that had engraved on it these words:

> AND IN THE SWEEPING
>   OF THE WIND YOUR EAR
> THE PASSAGE OF THE ANGELS
>   WINGS WILL HEAR
> AND ON THE LICHEN-CRUSTED
>   LEADS ABOVE
> THE RUSTLE OF THE ETERNAL
>   RAIN OF LOVE.

⌘

Not long after I returned home, Michael sent me a newspaper article about Yaddo that had as its headline "Paradise for Working Artists—Saratoga's Yaddo Provides a Home Away from Home." I could imagine the rhythm of her scissors, even picture her expression, as she clipped it out for me and put it in the envelope to send to California.

Truths about People

The Lost Airman

On the 6th of February 1943, my cousin Henry Sherman, the most beautiful soldier I had ever seen, disappeared into thin air over a place called New Guinea. I had expected this news ever since he taught me to sing the song of the Army Air Corps: "We live in fame, go down in flame, / Nothing can stop the Army Air Corps."

Before this, when he wrote our family from flight school, I had already begun to worry about him. One letter, which my mother read to us, alarmed me in particular: "Dear Folks, Flew like an angel yesterday. Things are getting tougher. I'm really learning how to twist that plane around the skies. . . . I like flying upside down best of all." It was clear to me, from the times my father had held me upside down, that Henry would become dizzy and be unable to steer his plane. After his graduation from flight school, Henry came home on his what would turn out to be his last furlough. My grandmother told him she was worried about his going so far away and began to cry a little. Henry took a silver dollar from his pocket and tossed it in the air. "My lucky silver dollar, Gram," he said. "It always lands heads up—see? I scratched my name on it. I'll be just fine."

He let me touch the dollar, then lifted me high on his shoulder while my father took a picture of us. The sun, glinting off the gold pilot's wings on the front of his hat, thrilled me and made me happy. Wherever Henry was, life was exciting. The brim of his hat was stiff, the points of his shirt collar were ruler-straight, and his sleeves had a sharp crease from shoulder to wrist. He gleamed with perfection, whereas my father, who did not get to fight in the war because of me,

33

because he had a wife and a child, always dressed in baggy pants, his shirt pulled out at the waist. My father's curly hair was wild and unruly, and sometimes he forgot to shave. Because he had an antique shop and worked with old furniture and dusty statues, his fingernails were always grimy.

Sometimes I wished that Henry, who was exactly twenty years older than I (we shared the same birthday, March 15), could be my father. He knew what I needed. He promised to send me presents from wherever he landed his plane in the world, from every base, from every far-away city. "I will think of you wherever I go," he told me, kissing my cheek hard with his beautiful lips. "I will send you dolls and fans and little bells and carved peacocks with great colorful tails."

I was four, almost five, and I adored him. Our mothers were sisters, although his mother, Eva, was twelve years older than mine and was born from a different father. She was tall and very magnificent. She wore great white corsets with laces and hooks and had no hesitation in pulling off her dress in front of me if she chose to, making me look at her flesh, the garters with which she held up her stockings, her shimmering large breasts. My own mother was thin and modest. She dressed with her face and half her body in the closet, letting me see only the curve of her bare back. Sometimes she even carried her nightgown into the bathroom to put it on.

The third sister, my Aunt Greta, born two years after my mother, had no husband, no children, and she lived in the house in Brooklyn with my mother, father, grandmother, and me because she had no choice and nowhere else to go.

Aunt Eva lived not in Brooklyn but in the Bronx, not in a house with a backyard and a front garden but in a tall apartment building with a marble foyer and an elevator. Her husband, my Uncle Eddie, had been a prizefighter. Though he was short and very solid, he didn't scare me, even with his broken nose. In addition to Henry, they had two other sons, Irving and Freddy, one older than Henry, one younger. All three were handsome and fun to be with, and I was proud to be related to them.

❦

The war, to a child in Brooklyn in the 1940s, meant several specific things: you were not allowed to interrupt a news broadcast, especially if your father tilted his head toward the radio and held up his hand to stop you from speaking; you were encouraged to make balls out of silver foil from chewing gum wrappers and discarded cigarette packs found in the street; and you were urged to give up any costume jewelry or beads that you had in your jewel box. The tinfoil balls would in some way help our boys win the war, whereas the beads and rings could be traded for food to the wild men of New Guinea should our boys happen to crash-land in the mountains and need to barter with the natives. All children were urged to buy war stamps for twenty-five cents each, to be pasted in a little book. Eventually, when the book was filled up, a war bond could be purchased. This would also help win the war.

Winning the war was what we had to do in order for Henry to come home safe and be with us again. Fighting the war meant that we had to draw black curtains over our windows when the blackout alarm was sounded. Giving up new leather shoes, eating lamb chops, and sugar to make cakes would mean there was more for the boys to have. It was all quite simple. If we did those things, Hitler would be destroyed.

⌦⌫

After Henry's disappearance, my family waited for news, any kind of news except a telegram. The fact that Henry had disappeared was bad enough, but everyone in my family and in my house was certain he was alive, which was good. The sight of telegram boys on bicycles was dreaded by everyone throughout our neighborhood, for they had the power to deliver the worst news of all: that someone's son had been killed and would never come home.

Mothers whose sons were killed in the war were given gold stars to paste in their window, just as I (who was in kindergarten) was awarded a gold star when I knew my numbers or colors or could tell the correct time on the clock in the classroom. My Aunt Eva did not get a gold star for two reasons: one was that Henry was not proven dead, only "missing in action"; another (I assumed) was that she had no window facing on the street on which to paste a gold star. Privately I wondered if she might want to move to a one-story house (preferably in Brooklyn, near us) to display her star if the telegram boy were ever to deliver the worst news of all.

‍ Lost boys were not new to our family. I already had one lost uncle, my mother's older brother, Sam, who my grandmother felt certain was still alive. Now her daughter had a missing son, too. I imagined that someday I would probably also be required to have a missing son, something I did not look forward to, although I recognized that it brought you a great deal of attention and visitors and phone calls and allowed you to go to your room to cry because you were having "a very hard time of it." Everyone in my house did a great deal of crying.

My grandmother, from the time her son was lost, long before I was born, insisted on leaving the front porch lit every night because she expected Sam to come walking in the door. She consulted fortune-tellers as to his whereabouts. She took part in seances. Others in the family just presumed he had drowned. He had gone fishing with friends on the eve of Yom Kippur—in a storm, no less—a very bad time to have an outing, since (as my Aunt Greta explained to me) that was the night all Jews were required to begin twenty-four hours of fasting to atone for their sins. Sam should have been in *shul,* praying to God.

I could understand the lure of fishing. My father often took me, in a rowboat in Prospect Park or on a pier at Sheepshead Bay, but we never went at night. What would be the point? How then could we see the sunshine on the water, the silvery dance of the fish on the line, the desperate struggle of its flapping fins on the wooden floor of the boat or pier, the heaving of its gills as it gasped for air, its final scaly stillness after it gave up the fight at last?

My mother told me that after her brother disappeared on that stormy Yom Kippur night, she—though only seventeen—had been summoned many times to the morgue to look at the faces of drowned men in case one of them might be Sam. My grandmother could not be asked to do it, nor could Aunt Greta. When I begged my mother to describe what the dead men looked like, she refused. But she assured me that, even though the $1,000 insurance policy would have paid off the mortgage on the house if one of the dead mean turned out to be Sam, she was glad none ever did.

Between my grandmother still thinking Sam would come marching in the door, and my Aunt Eva was certain Henry would hike out of the mountains in New Guinea and phone her from somewhere, I felt thankful my father came from a family of no missing sons and had no expectations that ghosts would appear at the door. Now and then he threatened to join up and fight in the war because he felt useless not being "over there"—but my mother and I begged him to remember how much we needed him over here.

⸎

In the weeks following Henry's disappearance, my Aunt Eva came over many Friday nights with her boys Freddy and Irving—really they were men—to share my grandmother's boiled chicken and kreplach soup. (Uncle Eddie still played poker with his cronies on Friday nights, though Aunt Eva said he had gone to pieces since Henry was missing and would never be the same.) After dinner, as soon as we all got to talking, Aunt Eva would take from her purse the letter written by Henry's commanding officer and read it to us once again to prove there was still hope:

> Dear Mrs. Sherman:
> How it pains me to write you this, the saddest duty of my life. Your son was a fine young man, a good friend of mine. I knew of his devotion to you. . . . All I can do now is tell you what we know happened on the 6th day of February, 1943. On that day we took a flight of our ships to Uau, New Guinea. Six in all. Over the Uau airport we were attacked by about forty Zeros and some Bombers. Henry was flying a ship called "Early Delivery" with Lt. R. H. Schwensen, Cpl. Erickson, Private Faun and Private Piekutowski. The Zeros came in fast and four were diving at Henry's ship. He went near the airport in a turn and from then on—no one is sure. It's not anything to help your feelings, but the Japs lost 26 in this fight to (I am sorry to say) our one. In this land of thousands of miles of jungles, mountains, and God knows what, anything is possible. But all we can do is look and try to find his ship. . . . As long as we are in New Guinea—we'll be looking.

These letters are harder to write than the war — Henry was my friend and Buddy — and if there is any way to find him, we will do it. You can rest assured in that.

Yours sincerely,
Robert. L. Ward,
Captain, 33rd Troop Carrier Squadron

⚬∞⚬

Through the War Department, Aunt Eva had managed to get in touch with the Schwensens, the parents of Henry's copilot, who lived in Wichita, Kansas, and now the two mothers began to correspond. Aunt Eva read us Mrs. Schwensen's letters, too:

Dear Mr. and Mrs. Sherman:

I know it will help you out to know there is another mother who had a son on Robert's plane beside us — her husband is a lieutenant in New Guinea. He talked to a native down there and the native said he knew where Robert's plane was and so they have sent a group of natives to map out a way for the investigators to get in, as the area is very remote and the jungle there is very dense. Her husband said at the time of their flight, they were carrying food as cargo, so if the boys weren't hurt, they'd be able to exist quite a while on the food which was aboard. He also said that they don't think the boys are prisoners of the Japanese because of the remoteness of the area where the plane went down. I am glad you have so much faith and courage, because I really think that in itself will help the boys wherever they are. This gives all of us added hope that the boys will ultimately be reached by this rescue group and trust by now that we will hear something definite and that they are all well. Should we hear further shortly we will give you the information providing you do not hear before we do, With best wishes we are,

The Schwensens.

"So anything is still possible," said my Aunt Greta.

"Anything is possible," agreed my mother. "And if there is any way to find him, they will."

"I know he'll come back," I added, though I was not sure at all.

It was that same night my cousin Freddy announced to Aunt Eva that he had gone downtown to enlist.: "I'm going to train as a navigator. I told them I want to be sent to the Pacific. I'm going to get the bastards that got my brother."

"Oh please!" Aunt Eva cried. "Don't do that to me."

∞

By August 1943, when Freddy had been shipped out to the European theater with the 82nd Airborne, my Aunt Eva got another letter:

Dear Mr. and Mrs. Sherman:

On July 5, Jimmie Campbell, who is now a captain, and who had been in the South Pacific area for nearly fifteen months, returned home from New Guinea. He was the leader of the flight on February 6th when Robert's and Henry's transport was apparently lost. He came to our home and talked to us a long time. He does paint a very dark picture for us as to the boys' safety. Of course, he was also giving us the Government's viewpoint as to their being lost and, as you already know, the Government does not hold much hope for the boys' safety. Nevertheless, they also do not have sufficient proof. The boys could still be safe because the plane has not been found. He explained all matters in detail as to how it happened that fateful day. He said they all really expected to be shot down when the enemy appeared on the scene that day. Anti-aircraft fire from our ground forces and fighter planes shot down twenty-eight Zeros out of about thirty-eight that day; but two Zeros broke through somehow and pounced on our boys' plane and apparently they were the victims.

We want to quote to you from a letter from our eldest son, who is training in this country as a pilot, as follows: "I have thought over and over again many times the conversation Robert and I had in San Antonio, when he said that he knew just what to do in case he was face to face with a situation . . . he said he would use his demolition equipment to destroy his plane after every body had taken to the parachutes. This is the reason they haven't found his plane. It had secret radar equipment which he swore to destroy before crashing. He had rehearsed this action over so many times in his mind that it was just part of him. I just know that he is alive somewhere."

So you see we have not given up hope as yet and we do not want you to either. Still trusting and hoping for the safe return of all our boys missing. With best wishes we are,

Bess and Justus Schwensen.

Freddy sent me an embroidered silk blouse from Belgium with a matching skirt whose bodice laced up high at the waist, and a china doll I named Alice, for whom my Aunt Greta made a head of hair out of black wool. I could braid this hair, though it wasn't as good as the blonde hair on the heads of certain dolls my friends had, the sort of doll that cost too much for my parents to buy.

Aunt Greta joined the Red Cross and spent days at the synagogue, making bandages out of gauze and knitting socks for the boys overseas. I often went with her, sitting at long tables with other women who rolled gauze and knitted socks. If sheets of loose tinfoil had been brought in, I was given the job of adding them to the growing silver ball whose purpose in the war effort I didn't exactly understand, though a silver ball as big as a basketball was an impressive thing to see. My mother had begun to save the grease from cooked bacon in a tin can, although as Jews we were not supposed to eat bacon. My father hated the smell of it; my mother said the grease oiled the tanks and therefore she intended to cook it every day, her contribution to winning the war.

My cousin Freddy's plane was shot at over France. He got an arm- and a legful of shrapnel and had to be shipped home to a hospital. My Aunt Eva cried tears of joy and seemed oddly happy that her son's leg was infected and full of holes. When they cut out the seventy-seven little pieces of metal, she put them in a velvet case in her jewel box where she also kept Henry's medals, the Distinguished Flying Cross and the Purple Heart. Whenever we went to visit her in the Bronx, she let me hold the medals, which were cold, brown, and hard and did not seem like much of a present if you were never going to come home again.

The war was lasting so long it was making everyone crazy. Every time we went shopping and passed the house of Mrs. Carp on East Fourth Street, we stopped to contemplate the four gold stars in her front window. Aunt Greta always said to my mother, "My God, my God, how does she keep living?" And then we had to do the ordinary things, walk on to the bakery and the butcher and the drugstore.

Suddenly, though, when no one expected the war would ever end, the war ended. People rushed into the street, screaming and tossing confetti in the air. Strangers lifted me into the air and kissed me. I never saw so much love in my life. I felt proud that all this happiness had something to do with my work on the silver-foil balls.

⟢◈⟣

In November 1945, a neighbor told my Aunt Greta that an article had appeared in the *New York News* on November 12 titled "Lindy over Shangri-La." The article reported that Charles Lindbergh had discovered some American planes on a mountain top in New Guinea. Aunt Greta wrote at once to the newspaper, asking for a copy of the article. The paper replied: "We regret to say that our supply of copies of that paper has been depleted. According to the article, however, Charles Lindbergh flew low over an isolated spot in the New Guinea jungle and discovered a primitive valley in Dutch New Guinea. There he saw three C-47 transports, an A-20 attack bomber, a Douglas dive bomber and two British planes which had made emergency landings and had been stranded because they could not take off in the rarefied air on a short runway. You may address Mr. Lindbergh in care of the Ford Motor Company, Detroit, Michigan."

My aunt wrote at once to Lindbergh and begged him to reply, to reveal, if he only could, that perhaps—by some great good fortune—her nephew was a survivor of one of those forced landings.

She watched out the window for the mailman every day, praying at the same time that the telegram boy would never stop anywhere on our block. She told me that Lindbergh, a brave man and a famous flier, had also lost a son a long time ago, a baby boy who was stolen from his crib by a murderer. She knew that if the letter got to him, he would answer it. She knew he would understand what our family's pain was like.

When the letter came two weeks later, my aunt opened it as if she were unwrapping a precious jewel. She read us every word:

> The Tompkins House
> Long Lots Road
> Westport, Conn.
> December 4, 1945

Miss Greta Sorblum
405 Avenue "O"
Brooklyn 30
New York, New York

Dear Miss Sorblum:

   I am extremely sorry to have to tell you in reply to your letter, that the newspaper report about my seeing an isolated place in New Guinea, cut off from communications, where several planes had made forced landings is untrue as are so many similar stories printed these days.

   I want you to know that you have my deepest sympathy in your great concern for your nephew who has been reported missing. I wish I had information which might be of value to you.

   Sincerely,
   Charles Lindbergh

Forty years later, when I was living in California with children of my own, I had occasion to travel to Miami Beach. Aunt Eva was living then in one room of a decrepit 1920s retirement hotel on Collins Avenue, a block from the beach. She had lost the voluptuous flesh that had made her seem bigger than life when I was a little girl and now appeared to me as if she had slowly vanished over the years.

She was waiting for me on the front porch. The minute we got to her room, she pressed upon me everything she could think of that was hers to give: an old slice of French toast wrapped in tinfoil that she had been planning to reheat in the toaster, a little china lamb that sat on top of her television, a nylon sweater beaded with pearls that she thought would look good on me at a formal dinner I was to attend that evening. She insisted I eat a big round cookie she had been saving in her tiny refrigerator, the kind of cookie we, as kids, used to call a "black and white."

Both her husband and her eldest son, Irving, were long dead. My grandmother and my father were also dead. Her son Freddy, a successful investment broker, lived two thousand miles away.

When we began to talk of Henry, she told me that his best buddy had married Henry's girlfriend; together they'd had three children. "Everyone is gone. Uncle Eddie. Irving. Sam. My mother and my father. It's all like a dream."

"I always thought it so strange that Sam and Henry were *both* lost," I said. "Two boys in one family."

"Sam wasn't lost. He was killed."

"He was *killed*? I thought he drowned in a fishing accident."

"No. Sam and his friends weren't going fishing that night. They were running rum up and down the coast. They were making a lot of money at it. Sam always had an eye for the quick buck. There was a rival boat that was stealing their business. They fired on each other. The Coast Guard got involved, who knows. Both boats were shot down. They both sank. No one survived."

"Grandma always thought he would still come home."

"We all think what we have to think," Aunt Eva said.

Before I left, my aunt and I looked through some old photos and came upon the one of Henry holding me on his shoulder at his last furlough: I am four, going on five, wearing a sweater and overalls and a knit hat with a pompom on it. My small hand is wrapped around the back of Henry's neck, and he—in his starched uniform, his Air Corps hat with his pilot's wings above the brim— shines resplendent.

Aunt Eva said, "I want you to have Henry's things—his letters from flight school, the picture album he sent me that shows him posing with all his airplanes and his buddies, the letter from his commander after he was lost, the letters from the Schwensens. Take good care of them. Tell your children so they know what happened."

⚬⚬⚬

In 1989, a little more than a year after my Aunt Eva died at the age of 92, my husband and I were having coffee and browsing through the *Los Angeles Times* when a back-page article caught my eye:

AIRMAN BURIED 46 YEARS AFTER DEATH IN JUNGLE

Leavenworth, Kansas—Nearly half a century ago, a young Army airman left his wife and family in Wichita to fight in World War II over the Pacific Ocean. On Friday, 1st Lt. Robert Schwensen was finally laid to rest here, a year after his remains were discovered by Australian gold prospectors atop a mountain in a dense jungle of

New Guinea. Schwensen and four other men aboard a C-47 had been listed as missing in action since their aircraft was shot down by Japanese fighter planes in February, 1943. Schwensen was buried Friday under overcast skies with an honor guard and a 21-gun salute at Ft. Leavenworth's National Cemetery. "At last he's going to finally be home where he belongs," said June Rockhill, the woman Robert Schwensen left behind in the fall of 1942. She was 18 at the time and had been married just three months. . . . Air Force officials in Washington said it is rare to find the remains of missing servicemen so long after World War II.

"Robert Schwensen!" I cried out. "Oh my God! I've got to call my cousin Freddy."

Freddy immediately called the Defense Department and learned that Henry's skeletal remains had been found, in the pilot's seat on the left side of the transport plane's cockpit. His dog tags were still around his bones, with his belt, his knife, his eyeglass frames, and his lucky silver dollar lying nearby. Robert Schwensen's body was also in the cockpit, on the right side. The bones of the other three airmen were intermingled in the back compartment of the plane. The government had been unable to locate any of the missing boys' families, and it was only when news of the plane's discovery appeared in a newspaper that a Schwensen relative living in California called for more information. Finally the family had been able to claim the body of their boy.

Freddy called me back the next day, hardly able to suppress the tears in his voice, to report that Henry would now be buried, with full military honors, in Arlington National Cemetery. The government was sending him Henry's lucky silver dollar and the few other personal effects that had survived the ravages of the years. Freddy said he was glad his mother had not lived to hear the news: "To know that they found my brother would have killed her."

After much searching through the phone book and making calls, I managed to find the address of E. W. "Swede" Schwensen, Robert Schwensen's brother, and sent him news that we were part of Henry's family and that we, too, had discovered our boy's remains. He wrote me back at once:

We just returned this week from Ft. Leavenworth National cemetery where Lt. Robt. H. Schwensen was buried six plots from his older brother Capt. Justus Schwensen, a B-24 pilot killed over Hamburg, Germany. Our family also lost a third brother, Lt. Richard Schwensen (Infantry) killed at Remagen Bridge in Germany and is buried in the American Cemetery in Luxembourg. Mother and Dad are deceased, but my younger brother and myself attended Robert's funeral. . . . It's nice to have all this behind us now so that we can go on with our lives.

A three-star family, I thought to myself. How did they bear it?

I did not go to Henry's funeral, but, one day when my grown daughters were in the garage looking through some of their old childhood toys, they unearthed a box of gold paper stars. I took one of them and pressed it in the corner of my bedroom window—my small salute to Henry, the most beautiful soldier I had ever known.

The Treasures We Held

My father, when he was still full of hope, believed in total security. One summer, just before we left to take a car trip from Florida to New York, he pulled up the worn carpeting in our one-bedroom apartment and placed white aspirin tablets under it, one every six inches—in a line from the front door to the bedroom—so that, when we got home, he would be able to tell whether the landlady had come in while we were away. Furthermore, he strung instant coffee jars along the inside of the bathroom door so that any crook attempting to use the toilet would crash against them and scare himself to death.

My younger sister and I, standing out in the hall where our bikes were chained to the banister, watched his bizarre preparations. God knew what he thought he had to protect. Was he worried about my mother's grand piano? Did he fear that the landlady was likely to give a concert on it? Or that a burglar would lug it down the stairs on his back? It's true he had reason to protect my mother's seashell collection that sat on the windowsill, and, of course, there was always my father's hallowed cigar box full of tangled necklaces, broken eyeglass frames, unset gem stones, an odd watch fob or pocket watch or class ring—the dregs of other people's estates that my father had bought in lots for cheap prices when he went on calls for his antique store. He hid this box—if he absolutely couldn't take it with him—in elaborate hiding places that we considered ridiculous. He reminded us daily not to dump the contents of the clothes hamper into the washing machine without first checking to be sure the cigar box wasn't wrapped in my mother's bathrobe.

When we finally drove away from the house (circling the block twice to be sure the landlady wasn't already hurrying out of her downstairs apartment and up toward ours with her master key at the ready), my father told us he had hidden his roll of cash for the trip in our Thermos, squeezed between the silver glass liner and the green metal outer container. At picnic tables along the way, while my mother unwrapped sandwiches for us to eat, he kept one of his large hands wrapped around the green Thermos as if it contained the crown jewels. If any of us asked to have a drink, he'd look behind him and all round the picnic table before he handed the Thermos over to us, waiting tensely while we hurried to pour juice into our paper cups and handed it back into his protective custody for safekeeping.

He wanted so badly to find treasures for us. Somehow, somewhere, in the 1950s, when we still lived in Brooklyn, he bought a large signed Frederick Remington oil painting. He had paid a hundred dollars and told us triumphantly he hoped he could get as much as two hundred. He propped the painting in its carved gilded frame on the bench in front of our house and let us examine it, a wild scene full of thundering horses and lowering clouds. Then he aimed his Brownie box camera at it and took a picture. When the film came back developed, my father's body was a hulking shadow nearly blotting out the unfocused painting, one blur overlaid above another. Later that week my mother sent copies of it to a couple of art dealers. I never did know exactly when he sold it, or to whom— no one bothered to tell me. It's possible he may have gotten even two hundred and fifty dollars.

⁂

In those days my mother had her own treasures, separate from and independent of my father's. His valued goods were always and only about commerce. Hers were connected in some way to her heart. My sister and I knew exactly what she kept in the vault of the bank on Kings Highway. She liked to take us to visit her side of our fortune whenever we happened to be shopping for shoes or clothes on the busy thoroughfare that I imagined had once seen the pageantry of kings. (For some reason, in those days, I thought all of Brooklyn was a kingdom.)

My sister and I would go with her to the underground fortress of the bank, past the armed guard, down the rubber-floored ramp, through the chilly corridor to the silver cavern where my mother pretended nonchalance as the attendant removed our drawer, disengaged the keys. We all acted as if we were not there to do the secret deed. I could see our faces reflected in the thousand gleaming mirrors of the drawers, keyholes where our eyes should be, metal pulls where our mouths should be. We locked ourselves in the small cubicle and laid the metal box on the shelf. My mother raised the lid, and there, rattling among our birth certificates, her marriage license, her father's death certificate, were the family jewels. There was the gold locket and a pair of diamond earrings that had belonged to my mother's mother in Poland. An engraved silver teething bell that was mine lay wrapped in tissue paper, as well as the two circles of blue and white beaded alphabet letters—my mother's name spelled out on both—that had promised us to each other at my birth; hers had been knotted on her wrist, and mine around my neck. She let me examine and try on her platinum wedding band, studded with tiny diamonds—it had become too small for her almost as soon as my father placed it on her finger. We came only to visit these possessions, never to remove them. My mother invited us to unwrap them, touch them, hold them in our palms. "These will be for you girls someday." It was clear she meant that my father would never lay his hands on them. And that was only fair.

When we left the bank, we were sure to wear vacant, dumb expressions as we passed the guard, our smiles just a little dopey to mislead the world, to keep strangers from knowing what we had, to keep the evil eye from discerning how blessed we were.

⌗

Pincushions were my father's great hope. He'd read in the *Saturday Evening Post* about an old woman who'd hid a million dollars worth of jewels in an old pincushion and her children discovered it by accident after her death. He was careful after that to be sure—whenever he bought out an estate—to ask to buy any sewing boxes, embroidery baskets and hoops, old boxes of buttons, silver thimbles, and mahogany darning eggs. If he was lucky enough to come away with a pincushion, he'd call the family to a meeting that night at the kitchen table, put his jeweler's loupe into the socket of his eye, raise his big pair of shears, and say, "Here goes, wish me luck!"

After I was fourteen (and we had moved to Miami Beach from Brooklyn so that my father could try his fortunes in a better climate), I refused to be called from my bedroom to witness the unveiling. I might be busy writing in my diary or talking on the phone to a girlfriend, and I didn't care to see the performance played out again: the fanfare, the light shining down on the puffy tomato, or the fat lace cushion, or the red strawberry, or the stuffed Aunt Jemima doll. I had no interest in witnessing the sudden slashing of the fabric, no heart to watch the sandy grit pouring out on the sheet of newspaper. Oh so hopefully did my father sift his large fingers through the mess, so thoroughly did he press each grain of sand between his fingers, making my mother do the same in case he might miss the single hidden precious stone.

I got tired of having my life interrupted. I already knew that the next day we wouldn't be shopping in Saks Fifth Avenue on Lincoln Road or moving to a house with a swimming pool; I knew I'd still be getting my clothes at Lerner's and my shoes at the $2.99 place.

My sister showed more respect for him. She always watched. She thought he couldn't fool us this long without someday having results. She had high hopes of wearing Capezios on her feet. She watched his little drama with her eyes wide and hopeful. She always patted his back when he rolled up the whole shebang and tossed it in the garbage. She always said, "Maybe next time, Daddy."

⌒∞⌒

The cigar box began to go with us to restaurants, to parades, to visits at the homes of friends. If my father took us to a cafeteria for dinner, he faced an exercise in balance and ingenuity. If the family went to the movies, the box was eyed with suspicion by the ticket-taker—how could my father explain it? He seemed to feel the hamper wasn't safe enough, nor was the freezer of the refrigerator, nor the shelf he had built just under the cover of the toilet tank. He owned a few real jewels by then, a few pocket watches, a few lapel watches, some wrist watches and good pins, things left over from his failed watch-repair shop, things people had left behind, unclaimed.

One winter, when I was home for the holidays from my college in north Florida, he called to me through the closed door of my bedroom to say that something special had come his way and he wanted to give it to me. If I'd been impatient in high school, I had become even more critical of my father since my college roommate and I had hit on the time-consuming and thrillingly betraying diversion of discussing how our parents had twisted our lives and ruined us. How could I tell my father he was controlling and manipulating me, that he was trying to buy my love and seduce me into submission by bribery? Since I wasn't even sure this was true, I came out of my bedroom to accept his gift.

With his eyes bright, he gave my mother the signal, watched as she pulled shut the curtains and put a clothespin where the cloth met so no one could peek in. Then, with the air of a magician, my father spread out—on a black velvet square—his gleaming collection. I was surprised at the beautiful things he was now buying and selling: real antique jewelry. He displayed his treasures before us: a French enamel pin with a miniature painting of an Egyptian princess on it (the band across her brow sparkling with tiny rubies); an oval brooch laden with irregular black pearls; a lion-head bracelet (the lions had rubies for eyes, a diamond marking each nose) with matching stick pin; and the usual nest of chains, both gold and silver, entwined like tarnished snakes, knotted from years of chilly embrace in the confines of the warped cardboard cigar box. My father could unknot those chains in a matter of minutes, working with two straight pins, poking and pulling them apart till the knots were magically released and the chains could be plucked up in long, free lines.

"And this is for you. Because you are working so hard in college." He held up a wrist watch, its face heart-shaped and covered with a heart-shaped crystal, its numerals made of tiny rubies. "It's been unclaimed all this time," he said. "So, it's yours if you want it."

"Don't you need to sell it?" was the only thing I could think of to say. I felt privately that I was much too old to wear my heart exposed in so explicit and precious a display. Still, his attention was upon me, his face so full of pleasure, that I turned the watch over to continue my appreciation. On the back of the case I read, in flowery script, the engraved initials: "V. I. F." To make it possible to want this gift, to allow it to be mine, I said to him, "Thank you, Daddy. I'll think of it always as being from my Very Important Father."

∞

Years later, after I was married and my husband and I had moved with our baby daughter to California, my father decided to make one more major move with his cigar box—along with my mother and my sister—from Florida to California, to be near us. He could succeed (or fail) in business anywhere—so why not in a good climate where they could play with their grandbaby?

He bought an old truck in Miami and packed it with his antiques. Like a family seeking the promised land in a covered wagon, they set out to cross the great country. My sister, a teenager and beginning to be slightly cynical herself, told me later how they had to pull the truck off the road every twenty miles in order to bathe the old tires with cool water, how my father slept in the cab of the truck outside their cheap motel rooms while my mother and sister slept inside, and how he guarded his treasures through the night, a baseball bat in his hand for security should anyone dare to threaten them.

In Los Angeles, he settled the family in a small apartment and rented a store on Melrose Ave. The familiar GERBER'S ANTIQUES sign went in the window, inviting fortune to find him. He stocked the shelves and display cases with goods brought not only from Miami but from as far back as Brooklyn. In the afternoons he left my mother "holding the fort" while he went out to round up new treasures. I noticed that he began wearing a heavy gold ring shaped like a horseshoe, diamonds all around the "U" of it. "For luck," he told me when I examined it, holding his huge hand in my own. "Your old man's looking classy these days, wouldn't you say?"

One of his first lucky buys in the new land was an original serigraph by the famous illustrator Erté—a print of a dancing girl leaping high in the air, jewels in her hair, her skirt, like a thousand dancing flames, shimmying about her bare legs, her breasts wrapped in three mere strands of golden ribbon. Beneath her flying feet, a row of hands clapped in wild applause, the flying fingers of men and women alike laden with rings and gaudy with jewels.

"I won't make the mistake I made with the Remington," he told me, knocking a nail into the wall of my baby's bedroom, where he hung the Erté with a flourish. "This one is to keep. It's for the baby's security. Think of what it will be worth when she's grown! She can go to college on it! She can travel to Paris, see the world, buy a car!"

"Thanks, Daddy," I said, hugging him and lifting the baby from her crib so he could kiss her cheek. "It's a wonderful gift." I thought he was looking so tired these days; his dark curly hair had lately become quite thin and gray. His legs were slow to lift him from the deep cushions of the couch. He groaned when he got up from the floor after sitting with the baby in a circle of her colorful wooden building blocks.

My mother, whose hair had gone white at thirty, seemed older in other ways. Worry had tightened her forehead. She urged my father to take it easy. She thought they should think about taking a vacation.

In the store one day, I heard her remind him that he'd always wanted to buy a silver Airstream trailer and see America. When would they do it, if not now?

"But how can we do it *now*?" He motioned toward the laden shelves and display cases, indicating the treasures they held, the duties he and my mother had as their guardians. "Besides,"—he gestured north to Santa Monica Boulevard, Hollywood Boulevard, Sunset Boulevard—"any minute the movie stars will start pouring in the door."

Movie stars did wander in. Robert de Niro bought an early-American red wooden high chair for his son. (My daughter had used it, and I had painted it red myself.) Barbra Streisand admired a Navajo rug and said she would send her housekeeper to pay for it and pick it up. When the young woman came, she told my mother that Streisand had given her instructions to ask that twenty dollars be knocked off the asking price or she'd do without it. My mother gave Streisand's girl the discount . . . and regretted it forever after.

When my parents finally did take a short vacation at the end of the summer, a trip to San Francisco, they came back fast; my father had begun suffering deep pains in his thigh bones. "All that sitting in the car," he said. But my mother knew this was different. She dragged him to a doctor. After a week of medical tests, at the end of August, he was diagnosed with leukemia. In September and October, his face grew moon-shaped from the prednisone he was taking. In November, he gave me his horseshoe ring. "I think maybe I wore it upside down and somehow it tipped the wrong way. What can you do? The luck just ran out."

In December, on Pearl Harbor Day, he asked my mother if angels were sitting in rows of chairs around his bed . . . and then he died.

⸙

"I've decided we have to sell what's in the cigar box," my mother said a year after he was buried. She was still running the store but selling only china and furniture. She was afraid of keeping jewelry in the store because of the danger of holdups. "Once I'm gone, neither one of you girls will know what those things are worth and someone will walk off with them for a song. I think we should go to Barney Fishman in the jewelry mart. Daddy used to deal with him, years ago, in Brooklyn and a few times here, too."

We were sitting in the kitchen of the small apartment, where, after my father's death, my mother had installed triple locks on the door and bars on the windows. Propped beside her bed was a policeman's antique billy club that she kept there for protection.

We watched my mother take the cigar box out of the freezer and set it down hard on the kitchen table. My sister flipped up the lid and idly stirred her fingers through the gold chains inside. *Barney Fishman:* I knew who he was. When I was ten, my father had taken me with him to Barney Fishman's stall in the New York jewelry mart. The man frightened me; he looked like a humpbacked villain, with his jeweler's loupe stuck in his eye as he peered into the depths of a diamond, with his crayon-black hair that looked glued onto his scalp, with his eyebrows that met over the bridge of his nose. I remembered how he had examined the gold cameo pin my father had wanted to sell. "What do you want for it—you think I should give you maybe a million?"

"I don't need a million," my father had said. He had touched the top of my head. "My daughter is my million, Barney. All I want from you is a fair price."

Now I examined the ruby-eyed lion bracelet, warming it in my palm. "Mom, let's try to sell to someone else first," I suggested. "Fishman is not going to do you any favors."

"Well, we could drive to Beverly Hills and stop in at Helga Weingrad on Rodeo Drive. She used to buy a few things from Daddy."

"Yes, let's, we should definitely start at the top," my sister said. "What can we lose?"

My mother made us pin the jewelry—in small plastic sandwich bags—into our brassieres. Since we were going out on the dangerous streets, she seemed to feel an obligation to carry on my father's high standard of paranoia.

When my mother parked my father's old Chevrolet station wagon on Rodeo Drive in front of Helga Weingrad's shop, I could see a diamond tiara in the window catching the light from the sun and sending it back in blinding darts of light. Other necklaces in the display hung on headless black velvet necks. We three women hunched over in the car, undoing the jewelry from our underwear.

"I don't think we're really dressed for Rodeo Drive," my sister said, glancing out at the passing shoppers. "We look like we just came over on the boat."

"You think Helga Weingrad didn't come over on the boat?" my mother told us. "And you said it yourself. What can we lose? We already used the gas to get here."

A buzzer had to sound before we could enter, and once inside we found ourselves in a small cage, waiting to be let through a second barred door.

"We have some jewelry to sell," my mother said to a young woman behind the counter. "My husband was a dealer who did business with Helga Weingrad."

"Follow me, please."

In a small mirrored room, we were invited to wait on hard red velvet chairs. An image crossed my mind from another time, another place—the three of us could be waiting to be processed through Ellis Island. A blast of strong perfume preceded Helga Weingrad, who swept into the room like a dragon lady, her red silk blouse gleaming, her old spotted hands covered with diamond rings.

"We have some personal jewelry to sell," my mother said. "I believe you did some business with my husband, William Gerber." As my mother spoke, I noticed that she had a yellow stain on the collar of her blouse and that she wore too much rouge.

"Then you know we only buy estate pieces," Helga Weingrad said.

"This *is* our estate!" The words burst out of my sister's mouth. As she said them, I could see, with a thud of my heart, the paucity of what my mother was laying out on the marble-topped table.

"We buy only *important* pieces," Helga Weingrad explained, reluctantly bending over to look more closely, but before she could lay her red fingernails on our precious bounty, I scooped it all back into the plastic baggies and dumped the jewels in my purse.

"Excuse us," I said, grabbing my mother's and my sister's hands, "but we've changed our minds, these pieces are not for sale after all. Please have us buzzed out." Helga Weingrad gladly let us out, breathing through her mouth. She wiped her hands on her immaculate white pants as we passed her by.

Back on Rodeo Drive, standing in the sun without sunglasses, watching the women with leather purses over their shoulders, gold hoops in their ears, and designer shopping bags in their hands, my mother and sister stood aimlessly, facing the Hollywood hills.

"So let's go straight to Barney Fishman now," my mother said, finally.

To see Barney Fishman bent over his table was like going back in time; he stood in the same pose I remembered, with the same crayon-black hair (or perhaps it was a wig by now), his back hunched, his eye buried in the powerful loupe.

When he saw my mother, he said, "So what have you got for me? I was sorry to hear your husband died, a very nice guy."

"I know I can trust you," my mother said. "My daughters need money—I want you to do the best you can, my husband would have wanted me to come to you. These are things he put aside especially for his girls."

"Show me what you brought," Barney Fishman said, and my mother motioned for me to empty out the packets on the counter. At least there were no mirrored walls here, no perfume, just the hard look of commerce.

Behind the counter, Barney Fishman flew into action. He held up each piece of jewelry, peered at it, tossed it onto his scale, and had it off in a second. He called off prices like an auctioneer: I'll give you thirty for this, twenty-five for that, no more than ten for that "and only if I buy the whole bunch." He rolled our treasures down the counter like a checker in a supermarket. My mother's lion bracelet rolled by for seventy-five. He said no one was wearing lions these days. He had an excuse ready for each of my mother's protests: the lapel watch was broken, it would cost him a fortune to put in a new movement; the diamond ring had an old-mined diamond, no one wanted them anymore. Pocket watches were a dime a dozen, sent over from England by the trainload. The pearl pin: if the pearls hadn't been black, if they were less irregular, if they weren't cultured, if they were set in gold.

"But this pin is gold, my husband told me so," my mother said. "And the pearls are not cultured. They're real."

"They're not real. And this is not gold."

"Get the acid, Barney, test it yourself."

"Look, I don't have time, I get busy this time of day. I'll give you forty for the pearl pin, take it or leave it."

My mother sighed. "I'll take it." My sister grabbed my arm and pulled me along the length of the counter. She pointed out how, in the display case, there were dozens of chains, pins, rings, many of them nearly identical to the ones we were selling. Every price tag seemed to read $500 or more. It was clear to us that tomorrow those prices would be on my father's treasures.

My mother's eyes were fixed on a girlie calendar on the wall. She was no longer listening to him. "Okay, okay, okay," she said, vaguely, to whatever price he was offering for the last dregs on the counter.

"So that's it? That's all?"

"That's it. That's all."

Barney began to add up the numbers on a calculator that printed on silver paper.

"I want cash, Barney," my mother said to him.

"Fine, fine." He was busy adding.

My mother leaned on the counter for support.

"I got a figure," he said. He held out the adding machine tape, and my mother glanced at it. "Okay," she said. "Okay."

"It's the best I can do," he said. "The way business is these days. So excuse me a minute, while I get the money in the back room for you."

My sister took my mother's arm and said, "Look, he has a ring in his showcase just like your wedding ring, Mom, do you want to see it?"

"I didn't sell him my wedding ring," she said. "Do you girls want me to? I could, you know. It doesn't matter really. Things are just things."

When Barney came back, he said, "I have bad news for you, Mrs. Gerber. I just made a quick phone call; the price of gold is down $12 an ounce from yesterday, what can I do? I was going on yesterday's price of gold when I quoted you. So what I have to do is take $200 off what I just offered you."

"Oh, that's baloney. A deal is a deal, Barney. In ten minutes the price of gold goes down? You know you aren't buying for gold weight. Some of those are one-of-a-kind pieces, they're rare antique jewelry."

"I swear to you, half of it is worthless. It's scrap gold, I'll have to melt it down."

"You got it all for almost nothing, Barney. Be a *mensch*. Do it for my husband and his girls. You're a rich man, Barney. You don't need this on your conscience."

"I have to make a living, like everyone else. Take it or leave it," Barney Fishman said, waving a thin wad of bills. "You'll never get a better price."

My mother reached for the bills and tucked them in her purse without counting them. "You have to live with your conscience, Barney, not me. Let's go, girls," she said. We marched outside without looking back.

After we got into the car, she said, "So now we'll never have to do this again. You'll each take half of this money, a few hundred dollars.

You'll buy yourselves something nice, from your father. And finally—we can throw out the cigar box. We can forget it."

∝

It was the next summer that a thought struck me. No one was home. My husband had taken our daughter to her swim class at the public pool, and I was putting some clean laundry away in her room when my eye caught the Erté dancing girl still hanging on the wall, on the very nail my father had driven in with his own hands. She wore jewels in her hair, jewels that seemed to dance in the light. Other jewels shone out of the picture—those on her headband, and those on the ringed fingers of her wildly applauding audience.

I decided to phone my sister. She was now living in San Francisco and going to college, but she happened to be home visiting my mother this week.

"Listen, I think we have The Pincushion," I said.

"What?"

"Remember Daddy and his pincushions? I think we have the Big One. I'm going to the library now, but come over in about an hour. Bring champagne."

"You've lost it, haven't you?" she said, laughing. "Okay, I'll see you later."

Among the oversize reference books in the art section of the library, I found a volume containing illustrations of Erté's artworks. I discovered, halfway through the glossy inserts, the picture identical to the one my father had nailed up in my baby's room. Yes! The very one we owned! Three hundred serigraphs were made of the piece titled "Applause"—each one numbered and signed. A footnote indicated that the lower numbers were the more valuable.

When I got home, my sister was sitting on the front steps . . . holding a clothespin. "I guess if we have the Big Pincushion we'll have to close the curtains," she said. We began to laugh, giddily, winding up for something. As children we'd had laughing fits in bed at night, though we both knew how dangerous they were. We'd pull the covers up over our heads, but, even muffled, our laughter would keep our father awake. By the time he was really angry, neither of us could stop. One of the times he stalked into our room, exhausted

58

and out of patience, and even after he slapped each of us, we continued to laugh like lunatics.

My sister and I went to work, taking turns with a small screwdriver, prying up the old bent nails that kept the backing on. The brown paper backing was raveled and water-stained.

"Here goes," I said. "It's free now, in one second we can see what number it is!" I began lifting up the cardboard.

"Uh-oh," my sister said. "Does an original work of art have an ad on the back?"

"It can't be. It must be another layer of backing."

"I don't *think* so," my sister said. "This is a single sheet of paper."

We were both staring down at what seemed to be a page torn from a magazine. On the side facing us it said *"Patrician Dresses, Shown at the Best Shops,"* and below were pictured two women dressed in styles of the twenties, one of them holding a Corgi dog on a leash. Underneath their delicate, pointy shoes were the words "Mannie Solomon Co. Inc., 31 East 31st St., NY, and 7 Rue Bergere, Paris." I turned the page over carefully. On the other side of the ad was printed the Erté dancing girl, dressed in her fingers of flame. Above her head and previously hidden by the frame were written the month of the magazine's publication, November, 1925, and the price of the issue: fifty cents.

"Well, Daddy said that my baby could see Paris on this—and there it is—the Rue Bergere," I said.

"Ah, the hammer blows of reality," my sister replied.

When my husband came home from the pool with our daughter, the Erté was back on its nail, and my sister and I were eating large bowls of coffee ice cream covered with chocolate syrup. My daughter, still in her damp blue nylon swimsuit, flung herself into my sister's lap, and the two of them began stirring the chocolate sauce into artistic shapes on the melting ice cream. My sister looked at me across the top of my daughter's blonde head. Perhaps we had the same thought in our minds. My father might even have been speaking into our ears: When a million lands in your lap, you know it.

Getting Mother Buried

In memory of my mother, Jessie S. Gerber

Twenty years before my mother was to die, she phoned me to say: "I don't want any transients at my funeral. I don't want all that flowery baloney in the newspaper: 'Adored wife, beloved mother, devoted daughter, cherished sister.' I want absolutely none of that. I don't want a bunch of strangers gawking at me, crying crocodile tears and coming back to your house for a party in my honor, stuffing themselves with food that you pay a fortune for and pretending they're heartbroken that I'm dead. And I don't want a rabbi who never laid eyes on me saying how charitable and good I was, the way that rabbi we hired made up things about Daddy."

"I'll keep that in mind, Mom," I assured her. "I'll take care of it."

My mother's song and mantra for the seven years she was in the nursing home—partially paralyzed and on a feeding tube—was "I want to die. I want to be dead. I want to be in my grave next to Daddy, I want to lie quietly in peace. If only I could die . . ."

Her roommates all had better luck than she; one by one they faltered, declined, were comatose for days, and died. One after another they were rolled out, to their peace, whatever it was to be. Each one of them had complained about my mother's constant wish—to die, to die. They were all waiting till Jesus called them, a pleasant convenience but one not available to my mother, who believed in nothing but the beauty and transcendence of music. She had been a pianist and now could no longer play.

I brought her tapes of Chopin, of Beethoven, of Schubert, of Tchaikovsky, of Mozart. I even bought her little plastic busts of all of them and lined them up on her bedside table—her little entourage of men. She'd always been a flirt, a woman who showed off her pretty legs by wearing short skirts. I'd sit with her, and we'd listen to the music coming out of the cheap portable player until my mother's eyes filled with tears. "It makes me too sad to listen," she said, time after time. "You better go now, you have things to do."

"Shall I turn on the TV before I leave? You could watch Oprah."

"No. I don't want anything. I don't want to think about anything. I just want it to be over."

And she'd commence to look at the clock on the wall, and I looked at it, too, that blank face of hours which she'd have to endure, one by one, till my next visit, or till she fell asleep, or till an aide came to turn her from side to side or change the feeding tube that pumped fluid into her stomach.

Every time I left my mother, I'd cry my way home. "I've got to get her out of this," I told myself. "No one should have to suffer this way."

My Mother's Suffering: you could say it was the theme song of my life. Shortly after I was born, she had all her teeth extracted. She suffered from migraines then—one theory was that "bad teeth" were causing her headaches. My earliest memories have to do with her retching in the bathroom as, after every meal, she removed her teeth to clean them. I never saw them, the teeth, the way I saw my grandmother's, sitting in a glass beside her bed. My mother's shame about her teeth was the reason she never smiled in pictures, the reason she found food a torment to chew, the reason she ran to the bathroom after every meal: I heard these sounds, her gagging and the sound of water running in the sink, all through my childhood.

When I was seven, and she was eight months pregnant with my sister, we were walking one day on Kings Highway in Brooklyn, and two young men, one chasing the other about some dispute, knocked my mother down in the road. I saw her fall on her face, heard her scream, watched her roll on her round belly from side to side before she was able to turn herself over. She had tears on her face as a man from the local fruit store ran out and helped her up, pulled her under the arms to an upturned wooden crate where he made her sit down while he called for a taxi to take us home.

Later, after the baby was born, my mother developed milk fever; milk had to be pumped from her swollen breasts. When she screamed, I had to run away, hide in my bed, cover my ears. It seemed my mother was always in pain; there was never a day she didn't press a wet washcloth to her forehead, that she didn't lie down with the lights turned off in her room, that she didn't beg her children to be quiet. As a child (who also sometimes lay down with a washcloth on her forehead, as practice for growing up), I thought that being alive might not be a good thing, not good at all.

Though it was not exactly my choice, I began to share her invalidism with troubles of my own. I developed heart palpitations; they came on suddenly, often when I lowered my head to pick something off the floor—my ball, my set of jacks, my crayons. I'd feel a crazy thump in my chest, and then the hoof beats of panic took off, thumping so hard that I could see my chest wall flop in and out as if a battle were taking place around my heart. When it happened in school, I'd put my head down on the desk till the teacher inquired, and then I was taken to the nurse's office until my mother came to pick me up. She'd have to walk fourteen blocks through the Brooklyn streets, often in snowstorms or in rain, pushing my sister Bobbie's baby stroller. I remember sitting on the wooden bench in the school office, a terrifying limbo, until my mother arrived, alarmed, in the doorway, pushing my sister. I'd walk home with them, my heart ricocheting like crazy, and then, within an hour or two, the mad thrashing of my heartbeat would calm. One last thump, and the quiet normal rhythm returned, like a blessing. I'd stay in bed the rest of the day, reading, sipping chocolate milkshakes that my mother would bring me, dreading that I'd be somewhere away from home the next day and it would happen again. All the years I was growing up, my mother and I had this in common, this knowledge that we were soldered together by pain.

⚭

When my father, at age fifty-five, complained of pains in his thigh bones, my mother convinced him to have a checkup. He hadn't been to a doctor in twenty years. He was the picture of health: tall, muscular, suntanned, not a gray strand in his curly brown head of hair. In fact, he made his living by his strength, hauling old furniture into his antiques store from the station wagon, dragging marble-topped armoires around, lifting cartons of books he had bought at estate sales (boxes of which he gave me to read as I was growing up).

No one expected a death sentence. We heard it with disbelief: leukemia. Galloping death. Within three months my father was dead, his eyelid and lips eaten away by disease. ("I'm a fatalist," he said to me one day in his hospital room, "but I'll fight till the end.") My mother was not a fighter but a giver-upper. I saw her give up at his funeral. I saw all the hope go out of her as we buried him in the rain.

My sister and I, just the day before our father's death, had bought a burial plot on a hill, high above a freeway. The two of us had gone cemetery shopping that day; we'd argued about the advantages of one cemetery over another: "This one is good, it's in a homey neighborhood, there's lots of cars passing by, it won't be lonely for him." "But it's too noisy. How will he get any rest?" Soon we were making jokes: "This one is near a playground. Daddy always liked to hear the sound of children laughing." "But the smog is bad in this side of town." We'd start laughing for no reason; we'd lean against each other, laughing, as we argued the suitability of finding a suitable resting place for our father in eternity. (He wasn't dead yet, not then, as we spoke.) We'd been terrible laughers as children, we'd laugh in our beds at night until our father came to quiet us. "No more laughing! That's enough laughing!"—and his words would send us into gales of laughter. He'd come back again—"Your mother and I need to get to sleep. We have to go to work in the morning. No more laughing!"—and as soon as he'd left the room, we'd start squealing again, choking with laughter till we could hardly breathe. Once (we both remembered this), he came into our bedroom after the third or fourth warning, and he slapped us each, very hard, on the thigh. We gasped in shock, and, when he had left the room, we turned on the light to examine the marks of his handprint, red on our skin.

That day, at the cemetery on the hill, overlooking the freeway, we bought two plots: one for my father, one for my mother.

After her first year of the seven she spent in the nursing home, my mother would ask us every day: "Do I have a place next to Daddy in the cemetery? How will they know where to send me when I die?" We'd reassure her: "If you die, they'll call us. We know exactly what to do, don't worry, it's all arranged."

A few years before my mother had the catastrophic stroke that paralyzed her right arm (it occurred in the hospital, where she had gone for routine tests!) and before she fell, five days later, from her hospital bed, shattering her hip and rendering her immobile for the rest of her life, she had been in my house, visiting us, having dinner with us, when she walked down the hall to my husband's music room and fell down a single step she had forgotten was there. She went flying (my husband described it to me—"she flew into the room"), landing on her side. Her screams stopped my heart; the sound of them had always been the ultimate torture to me. I ran in, and she was shrieking: "The pain, the pain!" I wanted to cover my ears, but I had to act grown up, had to call the paramedics. Two of my daughters were visiting from college. They huddled over my mother's body on the floor, listening to her scream. I wanted to beg them to run out of the house, not to take in my mother's song of life: her pain and her message that all was pain. My mother must have turned her head just then, to see me cowering against my husband, sobbing, and she said, "Oh, don't cry, Merrill. Don't cry." Yet, when the paramedics arrived and cut off my mother's clothes, I heard her beg them: "Why don't you just shoot me now?"

They stabilized her arm and shoulder, they carried her out on the gurney. In the hospital the doctor told us she'd broken both her wrist and her shoulder. The x-rays showed that neither one could be set. They gave her a sling, a splint, and a prescription for pills. She was crying all the while the doctor was talking to me.

"Please, won't you admit her? She's in horrible pain. You can't just give us a codeine pill and send us home!"

"We're not allowed to admit her under Medicare rules," the doctor said to me. "If she'd broken her hip, we could. But a broken arm and shoulder don't qualify. I'm not allowed to admit her with these injuries," he said. "I could lose my job."

For the next two nights, my youngest daughter slept on the floor beside my mother, who lay moaning on the couch in our living room. We spooned cooked rice cereal between my mother's lips. When she had to be walked to the bathroom, two of us would support her between us; her legs would buckle, and she would shriek if we moved her arm even a tiny bit. Her skin was waxen; her false teeth shone like stones in her mouth.

On the third day, I called a nursing home and said, "My mother has had an accident and broken her wrist and shoulder; the hospital won't admit her, but I can't care for her. Can you accept her there for a few days?"

They sent an ambulance. When the driver and his partner saw my mother's face, they said "This woman is in very bad shape; she has to be taken to a hospital." This time we chose another hospital. I phoned a friend whose husband was a doctor on the staff. He examined my mother in the emergency room and admitted her at once: "dehydrated, disoriented, in shock." He didn't worry about the Medicare rules.

After some days in the hospital, my mother was transferred to a nursing home. (Six months after her death, I read the little notebook my mother had kept during those days in the nursing home. Always organized, always with a pencil in hand: she had for years, as a young woman, been a secretary to two New York State senators, "Rabinold and Scribner.")

It is so cold in here . . . awakened by the "And then" lady, and someone yelling at her to keep quiet . . . I cannot bear it . . . there are 2 others that can be unbearable, too—the man who screams at night "Help, Help Police!" and the woman who yells when people are trying to sleep "Nurse, Nurse, don't let me die." It is so cold in here . . . I am one big iceberg . . . some person's TV, overpowering loud and deafening . . . Merrill, do you have my watch and ring . . . The pain is awful . . . They took me to activity room, it is a complete madhouse and I will soon be one of them . . . Dinner served, sent back the meat loaf, potato, vegetable, salad, sent it all back, got cottage cheese, canned pears, apple sauce, custard pudding, milk, chocolate cake, ate only a little and kept spitting it out, want to throw up. What will I do when I get home? Even the cottage cheese doesn't stay down . . . I don't even want to swallow . . . Earlier I tried to get glass of water from the side of the bed, I lost my balance and fell, sprained my right ankle and wrist . . . no relief from the pain . . . Merrill is my bag in your house . . . They left me in the toilet and forgot to come back and get me . . . I was screaming for help, banging on the wall, I couldn't stand up myself . . . they ignored me for hours . . . I thought I would die there . . . it is so cold here, I will freeze to death . . .

Thus began my mother's long decline. She stayed in that nursing home for a month, went back to her retirement home, had other emergencies, nosebleeds, vertigo, a transient ischemic attack during which she was unable to speak, lost circulation to a toe, which became gangrenous—and, unable to walk on her foot, was again admitted to a nursing home. After it was clear her toe was turning black and rotting, she was sent to the hospital for femoral artery bypass surgery; a vein taken from her hip was installed in her lower leg. The doctor said to me, "If she lives another year, and can walk during that time, I think this is worth doing. . . ."

My sister and I visited her every day, wherever she was, in whatever state of despair, anger, hysteria, depression that gripped her. We listened to her wrath, to her misery. Once, when I was there, they brought my mother lunch, broiled liver. "Meat meant for a dog!" she cried. "No one could chew this!" . . . and she tossed the plate of food at the wall. "This is no life!" she cried. "This is no life! Please children . . . let me die, I want to die!"

In the weeks following her hip surgery, my sister and I watched our mother suffer the pain of blood clots that lodged in her lungs, heard her babbling wildly in a state of morphine-induced hallucinations, and watched her protest as leggings, designed to contract automatically around her legs, squeezed hard, day and night, to keep her blood flowing. She was unable to eat but didn't quite die. A doctor spoke to us about installing a permanent feeding tube in her stomach: "She's hanging on by a thread," he told us. "She'll die if we don't put in a tube. If we do, you can't guess what troubles lie ahead;

it's a Pandora's box. It's possible that she'll recover enough to eat on her own eventually, and, if she does, we can remove the tube."

"Do it," my sister and I said. Her life still seemed of utmost importance to us. Though therapists came to visit her at the nursing home after her broken hip and her stroke, one to teach her to walk, one to teach her to eat, my mother, never a fighter, found the obstacles insurmountable.

With the use of only one hand, she could not hang onto the parallel bars in the therapy room, and the therapist soon enough saw the futility of trying to get her to walk. As for eating (something my mother had never enjoyed doing in the best of times), with the use of only her left hand, she was clumsy; she spilled food all over her gown and bedclothes. Furthermore, she could no longer insert and remove her dentures with only one hand, and eating pureed food in her toothless state horrified her. When aides tried to feed her, they gave her large spoonfuls, one after another with no interval between (they were rushed, they had many patients to feed), so that my mother gagged and had to spit out the food.

She gave up eating and depended for the rest of her life on the grayish-brown mixture that hung in an upside-down bottle beside her bed and was pumped via a plastic tube into a hole in her belly. Even that method of nutrition had problems; at one point the tube became blocked by scar tissue that occluded the opening in her stomach. Again, she required surgery.

On one of the days she was hospitalized for this new problem, I phoned the nurses' station from home and asked for a phone to be held at her ear. A nurse agreed to do this but left the phone in my mother's weak left hand, and, after the first few words we exchanged, my mother dropped the phone. I could hear her crying, "Nurse, nurse—I'm disconnected, come and hang up the phone." I held on, calling "Ma, Ma, I'm still here," but apparently she could not hear me. Like a voyeur, I kept the connection open, listening to my mother's hard breathing, my mother's sighing. Moments passed. Then I heard a small sound, like a poem, like a prayer, issuing into what my mother thought was her private space: "I wish I were dead. I wish I were dead. Oh, I want to be dead in my grave next to my husband."

My sister and I learned of a community group called Children of Aging Parents. This group was holding an open meeting at the local synagogue, and Bobbie and I, often feeling at our wit's end about our mother's plight, decided to go to see whether we might learning something about how to cope with her endless decline.

We were welcomed by two female "facilitators" and offered tea in Styrofoam cups. Eight visitors were present, only one of them a man, who said he was there to learn about "resources in the community." Going around the circle, we each gave a brief explanation of our problems. Most of them were the usual: not enough time, not enough money, not enough energy to cope with the demands of our elders. Except for Bobbie and me, the others still had parents living either on their own or with them; the problems were similar—parents falling down, parents needing to be taken to doctors, parents unable to handle their medications or forgetting to turn off the stove, parents emotionally demanding, childlike, sometimes vindictive, sometimes hateful. Bobbie and I, much further along in this journey, with our mother installed in a nursing home, felt, somehow, fortunate. She was cared for by others; we were no longer called in the middle of the night. We looked at each other and smiled.

Then, oddly, I sneezed. I sneezed and fumbled for a tissue and found I didn't have one. I reached blindly toward my sister, waving my hand to indicate that I needed a tissue. As she searched in her purse, she also sneezed! She looked up at me, her nose dripping, and I looked at her, mine dripping, and we began to laugh.

Incurable laughers that we had always been, we fell into deep waters here, laughing as we used to laugh as children when some particularly weird food lay on the plate, or at how the Jell-O shimmered on the spoon, or at how the chicken wings looked silly detached from the chicken.

Here, in a serious meeting about desperate troubles (in fact, one woman was just describing how her mother would fall whenever she walked to the bathroom herself), my sister and I cracked up. We were minus all self-control, had not even a semblance of adult maturity. We had merely to sneeze and we thought it was the funniest thing that ever happened on earth. We doubled over in our chairs, trying not to laugh out loud, but we were beyond help.

The facilitators, two kind women, looked at us with understanding but not much amusement. They paused in their discussion, no doubt believing in a moment we would get hold of ourselves and gain control, but their glances set us off again, and we grabbed hands between our chairs while new explosions of laughter shook our shoulders. We still hadn't any tissues, our noses were running . . . and now, also, I had to go to the bathroom.

I stood up and staggered toward the kitchen of the meeting hall, and my sister followed behind me. We were laughing so hard we could barely walk. I got a glimpse of the others in the circle, staring at us with disbelief. But it had gotten beyond us; my sister and I had been seized by some force that shook the laughter out of us till it turned to tears. Bobbie and I were racked with the violence of it, leaning against the sink, laughing and crying, but mainly crying, each trying to stop this fit, each trying to catch her breath.

My sister finally tore a paper towel from a roller over the sink and handed it to me. But I took one look at the little ducks on it and started on a new roar of laughter. We both wiped our faces and our eyes and our noses with the stiff paper toweling with little ducks on it. Nothing had ever seemed funnier to us in our entire lives.

As a last resort, my sister pulled open a kitchen drawer and lifted a corkscrew into the air, brandishing it at me. She glared, trying to threaten me into silence. But it was hopeless. We were not children of aging parents; we were lunatics of aging parents. We had lost it entirely.

My sister ran back into the meeting room, retrieved our purses, murmured some apology to the people in the circle, and hurried back into the kitchen to get me and led me, though a side door, to the parking lot. She jumped in the car, turned on the motor, and sped us away, burning rubber.

By the time she dropped me off at my house, I was almost too weak to walk. I struggled up the steps and rang the bell, too exhausted to hunt for my key. When my husband opened the door, finding me limp on the doorstep, he said, "It must have been quite a meeting. Want to tell me about it?"

The longer my mother lived, the further she seemed to be from dying. In fact, she rallied; she gained weight from the feeding tube. Her risk factors diminished as she no longer walked—and could not fall. If an infection was spotted, it was treated at once with antibiotics. Her physical health improved, and her mental health declined. Each time I left her after a visit, I was filled with unbearable sadness. I could not rescue her, could not fix her, and could not free her from her chains.

As the years passed, it seemed to all of us, including her, that she would never die. We had long discussions with her about this: she wondered, could we bring her a poison pill, could we shoot her? Could we take her out to the desert, leave her there, and let her die? She did not want us to go to jail; she asked us to call Dr. Kevorkian. The problem was that she had no fatal disease. Though her living will directed us to keep her from being resuscitated if her heart stopped and to withdraw heroic measures if she was dying, she wasn't certifiably dying. "Comfort care" directed by a hospice was permitted only if her doctor stated that she had less than six months to live. But, as we told her, she might live for years. To that she'd always say, "Do you call this living?"

Her doctor marveled at her tenacity. "I never thought she'd live this long with all that's wrong," he told us privately. He began to catalog her illnesses: some we knew of—the stroke, the broken bones, the circulatory problems—but he added new ones: gall bladder disease, ulcers, gastritis, arthritis, enlarged heart, Alzheimer's disease. (He was wrong about that; he had made an assumption, but he surely hadn't been listening to her.)

From her eighty-fifth birthday to her ninetieth, she received birthday greetings from the White House signed by the President. In addition, when she reached her ninetieth birthday, which came the day after Thanksgiving in the last year of her life, the mayor of the town in which the nursing home was located sent her a certificate of congratulations for living so long. Balloons hung from the bedposts when the family arrived with her birthday cake. The nurse had sat her up in her wheelchair. But on that day she had not enough strength to hold up her head, nor enough breath to blow out the single candle on the heart-shaped chocolate cake I baked. I blew out her candle for her.

She watched us with her burning gaze as we sang the birthday song. I knew she was aware I hadn't put the extra candle, "the one to grow on," on the cake. She had always been careful to do that for her children.

"Thank you," she said and closed her eyes. "Could you tell the nurse I want to go back to bed now?"

Something took hold of her then; an infection was starting in her lungs. The next day, as I arrived at the door of her room, I heard the sound of a suction pump and saw a nurse bent over her, jabbing a plastic tube down her throat as my mother thrashed and screamed in her bed.

Fluid bubbled up in her throat; she could barely talk. The nurse said, "We have to suction her every hour."

"Please, Merrill! I don't want this any more. Let me die."

A portable x-ray machine was ordered; the diagnosis was pulmonary congestion, that's all it was. Nothing serious. The suctioning continued for days. I had to run out of the room every time the nurse did it to my mother. I felt the brutality of it, the impossibility of her existence. She was a bug impaled on a pin. And I could not release her.

Then, two days after Christmas, the x-rays, ordered again, showed pneumonia in my mother's lungs. Within a day, her temperature reached 104 degrees. The nursing home director called me at home: "We want to send your mother to the hospital for aggressive treatment. They can give her IV antibiotics and put her on a respirator there so she can breathe better."

"No. Don't send her to the hospital. We'll be right there."

I called my sister. "I think this may be our opportunity," I told her. "We can tell them to stop treatment, no antibiotics this time. . . ."

"Do you think we can do it?"

"We can try." We sped to the nursing home.

My mother looked like a puff of air on her pillow. She tried to talk to us: "Girls, I want . . . I want . . ."

"What, Mom, what do you want?"

"I want . . ." but there was not breath enough in her to finish the sentence. I ventured to finish it for her.

"To die?" I asked.

Oh yes, she nodded, oh yes.

"Mom, are you really ready to leave us?" I asked.

Her eyes burned in assent.

"Okay, then. We're going to talk to your doctor. We're going to help you get relief. We're going to get you out of this, Mom. But are you sure you're ready to die? Are you ready to say goodbye to us?"

"Yes!" It took all her energy to say the word.

At the nurses' station, we called the doctor; the nurse, Bobbie, and I all spoke with him. He seemed baffled that we might not want the most aggressive treatment, "to use all the guns we have."

"She isn't going to last six months," I insisted.

He conceded she might not.

"Then why not turn her over to hospice care?"

I could sense his hesitation, but my sister and I pressed him—didn't he think it was time our mother be allowed to put up the white flag?

He finally said, "I guess we can call in hospice, if that's what you're asking."

"It's what *she's* asking," we told him.

He agreed he'd make the call to the hospice agency.

When I went back to my mother's room, I said, "Mom, a hospice nurse is coming tomorrow to help you be comfortable. You will have medicine to help you sleep. You won't be in pain. You'll just go to sleep and you won't have to suffer anymore."

"Today!" my mother gasped.

When my sister and I left the nursing home, I drove north toward the hills. Mount Baldy, in the distance, was covered in snow. A circle of golden clouds hovered just below the peak. "Just look at that." I pulled the car to the side and parked—we both watched the mountain darken as the sun went down. "We did it," my sister said. "Are you scared?"

That night, my mother was given morphine, by IV, by patch, and by droplets under the tongue. The feeding tube was turned off, and the oxygen cannula removed from her nose.

By morning, when we arrived, she had disappeared into the depths of her private inner space. We called her name, but she did not respond to us. We pulled our chairs close to her bedside, stroking her arm, touching her face. The hospice nurse had not yet arrived, and Pearl, my mother's regular nurse, was reluctant to administer the ordered infusions of morphine. She felt my mother's forehead: hot. "Poor Jessie," she said. She brought a Tylenol mixture and injected it into the feeding tube. "She's comfortable now," Pearl said. "She's sleeping peacefully. She doesn't need morphine now. Morphine depresses the breathing." "Yes, she *does* need it!" I said, and my sister added, "We don't want her to wake up." We looked at each other in the shock of what we had said. This time we didn't laugh. This time we were dead serious.

"Give her the morphine," we said to the nurse. "Give it to her now."

We sat with my mother all day, that last day of the year, my sister and I, my sister's son, my husband, my daughter who lived nearby . . . we talked to my mother, we played her Chopin's music, my daughter Becky sang to her. We declared our thanks and our love. But she was gone from us then—I watched her chest rising and falling with sharp little shallow breaths. She had almost got her wish. She was on her way to achieve it. And we were here to watch out for her, to be sure that nothing interfered.

It was New Year's Eve. The world was preparing for the end of the year, and my mother was making her way out of life. For hours, we watched her chest heave in little spasms of breath that kept her in the world with us. As it turned dark, we realized we hadn't eaten, we needed to leave. But we didn't want to leave her side. The hospice nurse advised us: "They don't like to die when the family is here. They feel your presence and they can't leave you. But why don't you tell her goodbye and that she's free to go? They say that hearing is the last sense to go. . . ."

So each of us spoke to my mother, and then we left her there. She drew her last breath without witnesses three hours later. The nurse told us that, just after she died, a great flock of birds was outside her window, crying in the trees.

∞

My mother had no transients at her funeral. No one cried crocodile tears. No strangers gawked at her. On the morning I was to bring her clothing to the mortuary, I sewed gold buttons on her soft red quilted bathrobe (the one that had little blue anchors on it). I wanted her journey in eternity to be comfortable. Bobbie and I brought the music of Chopin to be buried with her, along with an announcement about a book of stories of mine, based on her life and called *Anna in Chains,* that had just been published, We also included the program for the funeral, which starred my mother playing a tape of the music she loved on her own piano: "The Entertainer," a Chopin Nocturne, and "Sunrise, Sunset." We also buried with her directions to my house, for the party where no one she didn't like would consume the food I had paid a fortune for and where heartbroken was what we all would be.

It rained on the day of the funeral. At the chapel, the funeral director required that we look at our mother in the coffin, wearing her red quilted robe, and sign a form saying it was she who was about to be buried. I signed—but it wasn't my mother. She was already dispersed to the stars. We had no rabbi, as she wished. Each of us in the family said a few words about her, this tough-minded woman, our mother, mother-in-law, and grandmother who was so central to our lives. My daughter Becky played a tune on her violin, "I'll Always Remember You," and my daughter Susanna sang a Hebrew folk song. My daughter Joanna sent a message to be read: "She was glamorous: she wore skirts and elegant shoes and a pin on her collar. She was modern and decisive: she liked her hair white and short, she didn't like to cook and ate her meals out. She loved her grandchildren and let us know it. And we loved her."

On my mother's simple casket we had lined up the little statues of the great loves of her life: Chopin, Mozart, Beethoven, Tchaikovsky, and Schubert. At the gravesite, we stood as my daughters and others carried the casket to the grave, where my mother was lowered to rest beside my father, who had died thirty-two years before. The sky was just clearing, and fog hovered over the distant hills. We all shoveled the traditional three scoops of dirt upon her coffin. A friend recited in Hebrew the *kaddish* for the dead. We left my mother there, with my father. My sister took my arm as we walked away from the gravesite: "I hope Mom and Dad go dancing somewhere tonight."

"Look How She Holds His Hand"

A memoir of love in the fifties

I never knew the reason my husband's mother hated me so fero-
ciously when I was fifteen years old—a skinny, studious girl with no
ulterior motive other than wanting to be in love. Later, perhaps,
when my father sold her son an engagement ring to give me, I might
(if I'd been older) have understood her outrage, especially if she
thought something like bribery or collusion was in the scheme, but
at the time she despised me I had about as much conniving in me as
a firefly.

The summer of my passion with her son (it was brand new—
only a week earlier he had laid his heavy arm across my shoulder for
a picture with a Young Judea youth group we had both joined), our
family had to leave Florida to drive to Brooklyn to see my grandmother, who'd had a stroke. When, after being away for two weeks,
we arrived home after dark, I rushed to the phone to call Joe. His
mother answered and, after a pause, told me that he wasn't home.
When I said, "Will you please tell him I'm back and to call me?" she
replied: "I suppose I have to give him the message. I certainly can't
guarantee that he'll call you."

Easily moved to tears in those days, I cried. (I had already been
tearful on the drive home—a girlfriend had written me while I was
in New York and said Joe had been seen on the beach with another
girl in the club.) With his mother's voice still grating in my ears, I
heard a knock on the door of our apartment. When I opened it, Joe
stood there, in blue jeans and a white T-shirt, grinning.

"How did you know I was home?"

"I didn't," he said. "I knew you were coming back one of these days, so I've been taking the bus up here every night, just in case . . ."

⁓

He was never romantic, just dogged. He was handsome but had no sense of himself as attractive, so had no vanity. He was largely unaware of emotional dynamics (ours and everyone else's), and, when his mother prevented him from seeing me (he sometimes canceled our dates minutes before he was supposed to arrive because she said she had to take him shopping with her; she needed to buy him a new jacket), he would take her reason at face value. He never seemed to get angry at her. He did as she demanded because she was his mother and she wanted certain things of him and, because he was her son, he owed them to her. He saw no malice in her.

When he agreed to her requirements and, as a result, stood me up, my parents and girlfriends gave me advice: "Tell him you won't take this kind of treatment. Tell him you don't want to see him anymore; that will wake him up!" "Break a date at the last minute the way he does to you." "Tell him you're going to find yourself a boyfriend who isn't a jellyfish." I knew that, in Joe's case, no psychological tricks or threats could be applied and produce results. Any manipulation would simply convince him that I didn't want to see him anymore, and he'd stop coming around.

There was a heaviness about him, a heavy intelligence, a heavy-footed walk, heavy-lidded dark eyes, heavy arms that, when around me, seemed to push me into quicksand—I felt myself being sucked down. And manliness. He was, for seventeen, beautifully manly, with muscled arms and shoulders and dark curling hair at the opening of his shirt. When the Young Judea club went to a concert, one of my girlfriends took a photo of Joe wearing his white jacket and gave it to me. With his intense stare and a curl of hair coming over his forehead, he looked very much like—my girlfriend said even sexier than—Elvis Presley. There was something about the squareness of his jaw that spoke to me of secrets and passion.

And passion he had. Once our initial touching had begun (the arm over my shoulder at the picnic, the arm around me at the movies, the hand moving into the square neckline of my purple flowered

77

sundress as we stood in the back alley of the apartment house where I lived), he was quick to embrace me as soon as we could be alone. Sitting on the beach wall one night, he reached to touch my breast and said "Mind?" I thought he was saying "Mine?" and I said "No!" When he persevered, I was outraged. He was surprised, then confused. We eventually cleared it up and then laughed about it. After that, I never minded.

We had no car, no private place to be, no freedom from the eyes of our parents. His father was a traveling salesman, and his mother was left alone for weeks at a time. His father always owned a new car, mortgaged to the hilt, whereas my father, who was in the antique and junk business, always owned an old heap, sometimes two at a time, which cost a couple of hundred dollars and often had a missing window or a door that had to be tied shut with rope. Joe's father wouldn't let him use his car, but my father, knowing our plight, always offered Joe the use of whatever car we had at the time. He liked Joe, to the extent that any father likes the man who is sexually intent on his daughter, though, once, when we lingered at the front door too long (just outside the living room of our apartment where my father and my mother slept on a sofabed), my father opened the door, disheveled, in his undershorts, angry at what he knew we were doing on the porch. "You've had enough of that!" he said to Joe. And to me, "It's late, come in and go to bed."

On a night he loaned Joe his car to take me to the movies, we didn't go to the movies at all but parked the car in a vacant lot and spent it the way we had learned to, doing some things but never doing others, doing enough and never quite enough, making marriage, so impossible to imagine at that age, seem the only solution to what we wanted, which was to be body against body forever. When Joe finally tried to start the car, the motor refused to turn over. We were both gripped with terror that we'd have to call my father for help. We sat there for two hours more, staring out the steamy windows, hoping the God of Cars would bless us, unflood the motor or let the spark plug spark, and let us go home, unashamed.

In the interim, we did what we always did until the police came along and shone their flashlight in at us. Joe explained that we were stuck there. The policeman said, "Give it a try now," and the motor started, and the car moved, and we were saved.

We were only in high school then. Though Joe was in none of my tenth-grade classes (he was a year ahead of me in school), I had first laid eyes on him one afternoon as I sat in the school bus outside Miami Beach High School waiting for the bus to fill up with kids. Joe, whose name I did not know then, walked out of the school's back door carrying his books under one arm, turned at the gate, and passed next to the bus. His head came just under my eyes, close enough that I could have reached out the window and stroked his dark wavy hair. That's all there was to it—a beautiful boy and my susceptible soul. His flat-footed walk made me swoon. I watched for him each day after that but had no idea how I could meet him.

My parents noticed I had very little to do on weekends. When my father suggested I join the Young Judea club at the *shul* and offered to drive me there, I agreed, in my loneliness, to go. At the first meeting I attended, I discovered the flat-footed boy sitting alone on a sagging couch. When I asked a girl if she knew his name, she said he was "Joe," that he never talked to anyone, that she thought he was "very deep," and that he sometimes stayed after the meeting to play classical music on the piano in the big hall.

I was something of a pianist myself, if you counted the miserable years of piano lessons I had endured in Brooklyn and the endless hours of practice that never improved my technique. (One day when I was about twelve and had a lesson scheduled for that afternoon, I was with my mother at a shoe store on Kings Highway and walked into a glass door. It raised a bump on my forehead so large my mother thought I'd had a concussion. I can still recall my sense of ecstasy that I would be able to cancel my piano lesson.)

I did not speak to Joe, or he to me, at that club meeting. I stared at him till my father came to pick me up. Our true meeting took place by accident a few days later in front of my father's most recent business venture, a watch repair shop in the lobby of the Robert's Hotel in downtown Miami. On Saturday morning, I went with my father to "help out" at the store. The entire premises of AAA Jewelry and Watch Repair measured five feet by ten feet, with a window looking out on Flagler Street, Miami's main thoroughfare. My job was to take the repaired watches down from hooks on the wall, wind them, and reset them to the proper time. Winding watches was something I could do without much thought. I stared out the small window and watched people passing on the street. I thought I was dreaming when I saw the face of the "deep" boy pass by. He paused at a bus stop right in front of my father's store, holding a yellow Schirmer edition music book (the same kind from which I used to practice my Czerny finger exercises).

I dashed outside the store so fast I nearly knocked my father off his feet. "Hi," I said to the boy. "I saw you at the Young Judea meeting."

He looked puzzled.

"At the *shul*? Young Judea? You were on the couch? Do you like the club meetings? Are you going to stay in the club?"

"My bus is here," he said, just as it pulled up to the curb. He stepped up. "See you." And he was gone in a puff of exhaust.

I held nothing against him. Boys who were "deep" were not required to engage in lighthearted banter. In any case, I was already planning my strategy. When I got home, I began at once to practice my scales on the piano. The very next Saturday, when I saw him waiting at the bus stop in front of my father's shop, I rushed out, this time with a book of duets in my hand. "Hello, again," I said (this time the bus was not yet in sight). "Do you like to play duets? I thought maybe we could try one together at the next Young Judea meeting. I've noticed they have a piano there."

"Which duet do you have in mind?" he said, taking the book from me, opening it, and looking through it with some interest.

"I like the 'Berceuse' from *Dolly*. Bizet wrote it."

"We could try it," he said. And then the bus came and he rode away.

◈

My mother played the piano and drew sounds from the keys that belied her hysterias, her fits of screaming, her anger at my father (for investing and losing our few dollars of savings in some sham construction deal). What came from her fingers seemed the other side of the monster that came from her lips when she yelled at my sister and me about not hanging up the dresses that she had ironed (once she crumpled two of them into hard balls, our best pastel cotton dresses, and threw them against the wall of our bedroom). From her fingers came celestial melodies, the heartbreak of Chopin, the longing of Beethoven (especially when she played the "Moonlight" Sonata), the poetry of Schumann.

When Joe came to our house to get me for our various trips to the beach or movies, he and my mother would sometimes play for each other: she, dreamy, melodious, swaying to lives the music promised her, and then Joe, sitting upright, using his powerful forearms to bang out the rhythms of Bach, the dissonances of Bartók, the thunder of Rachmaninoff. I had no patience with either of them: I wanted to get going to wherever we were going, he and I, to our blanket on the hot sand, to our hot embrace in the movie theater. I felt the two of them were showing off, impressing each other and serving up compliments (while, later, they each told me of the musical shortcomings of the other).

Joe lived near the high school, in downtown Miami Beach, and we lived in Surfside, seventy blocks to the north, so nearly all our visitations took place in my neighborhood. On one afternoon, though, I had to stay after school for the meeting of *The Embryo*, the literary magazine, and Joe suggested I come to his house afterward and meet his mother. (I already knew his younger sister, who was in my geometry class.) He thought I should at last meet his mother, whose voice on the phone terrified me. He wanted to demonstrate to her what a nice girl I was, smart (the literary magazine), an A student, well mannered, polite.

She came to the door looking like a bulldog. (Later, after the engagement-ring hysteria, when my mother talked about her to me, she always referred to her as "Hatchet Face.") His mother said, "Hello. So you're Joe's friend who calls here so often." I sat down in the living room, and she sat down on a chair across the room; Joe sat down on another chair but a second later got up and went over to the upright piano and proceeded to play something loud and violent on the keys. His mother looked me up and down. She was short and stocky, top-heavy, with the kind of enormous breasts that look like a shelf. Her angry eyes passed over me like a searchlight, head to toe, and I could tell she saw nothing pleasing. Her expression was set: a frown. I had no idea how long Joe would go on playing and leave me suffering on the couch. When someone knocked at the door, his mother said loudly, "Joseph, see who it is," and he got up, midnote, and opened the door. Two women stood there on the stairs. One of them said, "We're here for cancer." Joe replied, "No thanks. We don't want any" and closed the door. His mother's mouth hung open. "You think that's funny?" she said. "You think that's *funny*? There's really something wrong with you; you're mentally defective."

Then the visit was over. Joe said he was going to take me home on the bus. His mother said, "You'll need money." It wasn't a question. She opened her black handbag and took out her change purse. She had her back to me, counting coins into her son's hand. "Will you need carfare for *her,* too?" she said.

"I have my own money for the bus," I said in a casual way, as if to no one in particular.

"You'll need something for a sandwich if you stay later," his mother said to him, not even glancing at me. "Will you be buying one for *her*?"

"He can eat at my house," I said to the back of her head. "We always have plenty."

"Are you sure her parents are going to be home?" she asked her son. "I know it's the girl's parents who are supposed to worry, but I don't want her getting into trouble and then you'll have to be the one to pay the consequences."

We went down the steps, we were on the street, I could feel the warm ocean wind in my hair. Joe did not seem to realize any violence had taken place, but I felt weak and almost wanted to throw up.

⌒∞⌒

The summer Joe was in his senior year (and I in my junior), we both had summer jobs. He worked for a brokerage company in North Beach, writing stock prices on a blackboard, and I worked in South Beach, posting mortgage payments for a mortgage company. Each morning we took buses that passed each other at some midpoint on Collins Avenue. I would always sit in a window seat on the side of the bus behind the driver, my lunch in a paper bag on the seat beside me, and wait for the glare of the sun on the wide glass windshield of the approaching bus. I held my breath as the other bus approached, getting my arm in position to snake out the slightly opened window and wave at the exact right moment that Joe's arm came out of his bus and waved to me. That was my nourishment for the day: the memory of his bare, hairy, beautifully shaped arm waving to me. I lived on it till the night, when I was home again, when he might or might not call, when he might or might not be able to get away to see me, when his mother might or might not have some urgent errand for him to go on with her. She'd decided to buy two small bookcases that summer. He went with her to a hundred furniture stores. She told him that, without his father there, she needed a male opinion to be sure the bookcases would "go" in the apartment with the rest of the furniture. His sister's opinion wasn't asked for.

In our own apartment we had only used furniture—whatever my father picked up in homes where he was buying jewelry or antiques or whatever he was trying to make a living with at the moment. By this time he had given up the watch repair cubicle and now had a bigger store in Hialeah called the Lucky Elephant Trading Post. He handled antiques and jewelry, and he was also in partnership with his brother in a fledgling upholstery business. In the back room there was always a man with tacks in his mouth, hammering cloth into the frames of old couches.

My parents watched me suffer nightly, waiting by the phone for Joe to call. They thought this anguish, inflicted upon me by a young man, wasn't good for me. I thought it was probably average for what you had to suffer for love.

❧

When Joe graduated high school, he went away to the University of Florida in a town called Gainesville, four hundred miles north of Miami Beach. I counted the hours till he would come home on holidays—Thanksgiving, Christmas, spring break. Just before Thanksgiving, Joe invited me to come to Gainesville for the homecoming game and dance. His mother had insisted he pledge the Jewish fraternity on campus, thinking it would be good for his social life. He invited me to a dinner at the fraternity house that weekend. Another condition of his being at college (of her sending him money to live on) was that he take golf as one of his physical education courses. His mother imagined that it would help him be more successful in business later in life. I begged my parents to permit me to attend the festivities with Joe. I could take the milk train—cheap— to Ocala, and Joe would borrow a roommate's car to pick me up at the station. A girl he knew in the dorms would put me up on the floor of her room. I would be gone only for the weekend, and it would cost almost nothing. My father was reluctant to send me so far away. My mother agreed to help me find a formal gown. She turned up a secondhand, out-of-style dress at an estate sale where my father was buying some furniture. It was strapless, pink, made of scratchy tulle, with a fake satin rose between the points of the bodice. When I tried it on—with my bony chest and skinny shoulders— I looked like a skeleton that had been lowered into it.

I knew this meeting in Gainesville with Joe would be a test. His letters had been highly unsatisfactory, very brief, impersonal, listing his classes, the concerts he had attended, and always concluding with the big sloppy loop of his name under the word "Love." This wasn't enough to sustain me. In my letters, I wrote him about the moon shining on my bed at night and how the same moon must be shining into his window at school. No trace of moonshine ever got into his letters. I began to think I had wasted my life on him.

The milk train from Miami was filled with babbling girls going to spend the homecoming weekend with their boyfriends, and the talk was all of gowns and hairdos and their hopes of "getting pinned." Eight hours later, when the train pulled into the station at Ocala, I fell off the platform into Joe's arms. All my doubts vanished. We could not let go of each other.

We dropped my suitcase at the dormitory and wandered the campus, our arms wrapped around each other, till dinnertime, when we had to go to the fraternity house and sit at a long table set with plates decorated with alligators, the university's mascot. At each boy's place was a silver charm bracelet with the three Greek letters *A, E,* and *Pi* hanging from it—and, by dinner's end, the date of each young man was wearing such a bracelet on her wrist. Joe put on mine for me, and, as the evening went on, as the fraternity boys and their dates played loud music, grew more noisy and boisterous, we simply walked out and found a bench on the campus and curled against each other without talking. We stood up only at the very last minute, just in time for me to get into the girls' dorms before the doors were locked for the night.

Language was not Joe's gift, unless music counted as language, so we talked very little that weekend. The next day, when everyone was at the football game, Joe took me to the music building and into a practice room, where he sat down at the keyboard and proceeded to play Bach for me—very loudly—deafeningly, really. His disappearance into music reminded me of how he had played in his mother's living room, as if to obliterate us by the energy of the sound or, failing that, to lose himself in it. I ignored the racket and concentrated on how the muscles of his back made his shirt shimmer as his arms moved back and forth along the keyboard. When he had played enough, we stood in the corner of the room, out of sight of the window in the door, and kissed.

That evening, I had to dress in my crispy tulle cocoon for the homecoming dance. Sprays of perfume from atomizers flew back and forth across the room as the girls who were putting me up tried to find the most romantic fragrance to wear. When Joe picked me up, dressed up in a tux he had borrowed, we made no pretence of going to the dance but walked instead to a diner in downtown Gainesville and sat on two stools at the counter. I could see myself reflected in the mirror over the toaster and grill—I looked as if I were wrapped in barbed wire. The red cummerbund around Joe's waist made me think he had been gored by a bull. We sipped a shared milkshake till some man walking past us said, "Nothing can be that bad, kids, can it? You look like two corpses. Cheer up."

⌘

During Christmas vacation, his mother, at Joe's insistence, grudgingly agreed that I could be invited to dinner at their house. Joe's father would be there, and Joe wanted me to meet him. His mother served baked ham (something we would never have had in our house), and she opened a large tin can at two ends and slid out a sticky round brown bread, which she sliced and served to us. Joe's father was a garrulous, handsome man, wearing heavy gold rings; he was dressed in a gaudy, patterned shirt and sharply creased pants. In the living room stood his sample cases, huge black cardboard boxes, with straps around them, in which he carried a line of children's clothes that he sold all over the southern states. Every remark he made to me during dinner was prefaced by the line "Sister, have I got news for you."

Joe's sister said only a few words: she complained she didn't like ham. The bridge chair was wobbly. She hated creamed spinach.

It looked to me as if she and Joe shared the same face. They could have been twins. But he had been born eleven months ahead of her and therefore had a double advantage: he was a boy, and he was older. Her response to being so limited by an accident of fate was to enrage her mother by dressing in large men's shirts and dungarees, refusing to wear any makeup, and never combing her curly hair. Joe's mother seemed afraid of her. Before dinner, Joe had shown his mother a list of his grades so far for the term—all As. Instead of congratulating him, she said "Shh, I don't want your sister to know about this; it will just make her angry." His sister was already angry at everything, all the time, and I admired her for this—it seemed a fitting response to her environment. I could tell she held me in contempt for being far too polite and passive, a conscientious "good girl" in the same way that she was clearly a "bad girl." (The following fall, when I attended the University of Miami because I'd won a scholarship there, she came to my dorm room and asked me whether I'd let her sleep in my bathroom because she wanted her parents to think she was out all night with a boy.)

When I offered to help Joe's mother clear the table after dinner, we stood briefly in the kitchen, and she said to me, "Joseph has years of education ahead of him. He's much too young to be making any permanent decisions now." I pretended I had no idea what she was talking about and went back to the table to wait for dessert, which was Jell-O with pineapple folded into it.

⟨∞⟩

Though my parents wanted me to keep my scholarship to the University of Miami, I implored them to let me leave there and transfer to college in Gainesville, to be near Joe. They understood how unhappy I was, parted from him, and agreed. Once I got there, Joe and I continued our endless, frustrated courtship, on campus benches, on the grassy slope behind my dormitory, in the student union and in campus burger shops. Once I went with Joe to get his mail at his P.O. box. He was out of money again. His mother sent him only $10 at a time, in letters spaced at long intervals. He was forced to check his mailbox several times a day during the times he was totally out of money. He had taken a job in the education library for sixty cents an hour, but what he earned couldn't cover his meals and haircuts and other expenses. (I wasn't one of them. I paid my own way to everything.)

On this day, he found a letter from her waiting in his box and ripped it open to see whether some money might be included. There was a ten-dollar check inside, which—if he wanted to eat lunch that day—he needed to cash in the student bank immediately. He left me waiting outside the bank holding his mother's letter while he took the check inside. I read the letter:

> Dear Joseph—
> Well, you certainly never write us — do you? — unless you are asking for money. It wouldn't break your heart to tell us a thing or two about your classes there, the people you are meeting (we hope!) and the social life you should be having with the fraternity. As we discussed, we hope you are not spending time with Merrill, since, as we told you, it is a very bad idea. Being as lazy as you are, you settled for the first thing that came along when you could do much better. She is taking advantage of you, as you know. She is not for you! Don't let this go on! Get yourself out there and find some new girls to spend time with. She's not worth your time. You'll thank me for it.
> Love, Mother

cℚⁿ

I had fantasies of falling in love with someone else: I'd pick a boy, any boy, and try him out in my mind. He would have a mother who loved and appreciated me. On my birthday, she would send me silk pajamas. In the summer, the boy's family would take me with them on vacation to Key West, and we'd all live in a cottage on the ocean.

There actually were quite a few young men at school who liked me, who had coffee with me in the student union, who walked me from one class to another when Joe was elsewhere taking his classes or doing his laundry or working in the education library. My confidence in myself was growing: I was surely not such a bad bet. How much better could Joe do, after all? Whom did his mother imagine he could bring home on his arm? A starlet? An heiress? But none of the young men who hung around me interested me; I was soldered body and soul to Joe as if we had been attached by the position of the stars, by cosmic prophecy. His shortcomings were irrelevant (those I counted seemed unimportant in exchange for his beauty). His unwillingness to be cruel or rude to his mother simply proved his goodness of heart. A man good to his mother would be good to his wife. His temporary powerlessness was only a function of our dependent situation. All he had to do was hold me on his lap under the canopy of a great tree, hold me and kiss me, and I was reset and rewound, the way the watches in my father's shop were brought back to life. We both counted on eventually demonstrating to his parents that we had a sensible, practical plan. We weren't going to elope or get pregnant or run off to Puerto Rico. We just wanted to be left in peace to see each other till everything was in place and we could marry.

∞

I dreaded the coming summer of my junior year—a summer at home with Joe at his mother's beck and call, with me waiting, disconsolate, by the phone. I told Joe we had to make some kind of a statement to his parents. Take a stand. Make it clear to them how determined we were. He understood the problem, it was not as though he were oblivious to it—but our long-range plans required that we both graduate from the university, and for that he needed his parents' financial support. If he angered them, they would— they had already threatened to—stop sending him money. My parents were surely not better off than his, but, at least, at the beginning of each term, they gave me a check for several hundred dollars to deposit in my student account and from that I paid for my dorm, my food and books, my occasional trips to the movies or a concert on campus. They never made me beg. They surely never wanted me to waver on the edge of destitution and fall on my knees to them. On the other hand, I gladly wrote letters to them, willingly and frequently, filled with lots of news.

At spring break, home again, and in the midst of a new volley of directives from Joe's mother that she needed him at home for various errands, I had the idea that, if we told Joe's parents we were engaged, they would understand the depth of our commitment and stop trying to keep him from seeing me. "But I have no money for a ring," Joe said.

"Maybe we could borrow one from my father. He has lots of rings." We consulted my father after dinner that evening. I could see how happy he was to oblige, to know that we might be taking a new and positive turn in the road. He brought out his cigar box of treasures—the full holdings of his jewelry business. He looked through the jumble of pins and rings and plucked out a diamond ring. The stone was brilliant and large.

"Go ahead, try it," my father said and handed it to Joe, who slipped it on my finger. It fit. "Well, that should do the job," my father said.

I could see Joe was uneasy about this strange transaction. If he was borrowing the ring, then when would he ever return it? He posed this question to my father.

"Consider it yours," my father said. "Call it an engagement present."

Joe said he would rather buy it, though he couldn't pay all at once. My father suggested a few payments on the installment plan.

"How much would it be?" Joe asked.

"How about sixty dollars? Could you manage five dollars a month?" So the deal was made, the two men shook hands, and I supposed I was engaged to be married.

During that spring vacation, a couple with whom Joe and I were friends at the university got married. They, like we, had courted on benches on the campus, had met for years in empty classrooms, and had been lucky enough to have even more private trysts in the office of one of Jerry's professors, who had given him a key to it. Their parents had taken pity on them and had agreed to support them in their married state till they finished school. Joe and I visited with them in the hotel room where they were getting dressed before the wedding. Paula opened the lid of her suitcase to show me her new honeymoon clothes, and there, in a long white box against the side, was a tube of Ortho-Gynol contraceptive cream, packed for its sacred journey into matrimony. I had to turn away and leave the room, to cry out my envy in the garden of the hotel.

We were going to make our announcement to Joe's parents on the last day of spring break. Our plan was this: we'd be returning to the university that Sunday morning, going with two of Joe's friends who had room in their car to give us a ride back to school. First, the boys would stop at my house and pick me up (with my luggage) and then drive downtown to Joe's house, and I'd go upstairs to get him. It would be in that brief moment we'd announce our engagement to his parents. I'd show them the ring. We would be very careful to assure them that we were going to finish school before getting married. Joe predicted that, given the element of surprise, they would have to congratulate us, since there'd be no time for argument or debate.

They would know the car was waiting for us downstairs; they would have no recourse other than to wish us the best.

I think we both believed this would come to pass. It was springtime, the world was abloom in fragrant blossoms, Joe had been freer than usual in getting away to see me during spring break, and we had lain for hours on a blanket on the beach, day after day, staring up at the blue sky and naming the children we would someday have. The ring on my finger seemed a guarantee that the future existed for us, that we would finally achieve it.

I don't know exactly what words we used to announce our engagement to Joe's parents. I have a memory of their mouths transformed into great holes out of which poured ear-splitting howls of fury. I wanted Joe to rush to the piano to drown them out. He did not but stood paralyzed beside me, holding my hand, while they cursed, accused, threatened, spewed their poison breath in our faces. If there was content to their shouting, I heard only a few words: "Look how she holds his hand! Look how she stands there, holding his hand." As if nothing could have disgusted them more, been more obscene.

"You go to hell," his father yelled at me. "You bitch!" his mother cursed at me. They chased us to the door and nearly pushed me down the stairs. Joe followed behind me, his heavy shoes skidding down the points of the steps. His parents followed us into the street, hollering.

We climbed in the back seat of the car and huddled together, while his parents banged their fists on the sides and roof. "You!" they screamed at me. "You're ruining his life!"

The two boys in the front seat looked over at us.

"Go," Joe said.

The car pulled away, and Joe buried his head in my shoulder. His body shook with sobs. The trip back to school took seven or eight hours. I recall none of it—just that we hid our faces and shivered with grief. When I got to my dorm, I took my suitcase and dragged it into the lobby. The boys drove off to drop Joe at his room. As I signed in at the front desk, a girl who lived on my floor spotted my engagement ring and began to shriek.

"Hurry everyone! Come see! She's engaged, oh my god, she's got a diamond ring!!" Pandemonium ensued. All the girls within earshot gathered to admire the object on my finger. As was the custom, a group of them surrounded me and herded me into the bathroom, where they shoved me, still fully dressed, under the shower. "She's engaged, the lucky dog. She's got her *ring*! Next she'll have her MRS degree!"

I hated the ring. It caught on my clothes, caught in the bed-sheets, hung on my hand like an iron weight. I wore it for two hours, then took it off and put it in my underwear drawer, under my panties.

When my parents phoned to ask me whether they should call Joe's folks and share congratulations all around, I told my mother what had happened. I cried. She put my father on the phone and he consoled me, said that maybe things would calm down and to remember that, no matter what happened, they loved me. Joe came around later that night and told me his parents had called him, too, and continued to berate and curse him on the phone. Twenty minutes later, they called back and tried to reason with him. They begged him. They bribed him. They offered to send him to the University of Michigan next year, to get him away from me, to send him to a better school than this one, one at the other end of the world from where I was.

"But you wouldn't do that, would you? Let them blackmail you?"

"I'll have to think about it." Joe said. "You know I was planning to go there for graduate school. It would be the best thing for our future. They have a very good sociology and history program there, just the kind I'm interested in. I'll really have to consider it."

The following weekend, Joe and I were in the library, studying. We sat at a long wooden table, our books open, while across from me sat one of my admirers, a boy named Harry. He seemed to be writing a poem and looked up at me from time to time. I ignored his attentions and tried to study. I was having trouble doing my schoolwork. I was often unable to eat. My stomach bothered me. When I looked at Joe, I felt sick that he so willingly would consider leaving me. I wouldn't have left him for all the enticements in the world.

I whispered to Joe that I was going to the ladies' room and left the table. When I came back, ten minutes later, Joe was gone. His books were gone. His jacket was gone. His chair was pushed in.

The boy named Harry was watching me. "Do you know where he went?" I asked him.

"He left with an older man," Harry said. "The man looked like him. He came and said something to him, and then they both left."

"Joe didn't leave me a note? Give you a message to tell me anything?"

Harry shook his head. "He vanished like a puff of smoke."

I thanked him and left the library and went back to my dormitory and got into bed, where I lay for several hours till the buzzer in the room rang.

"You have a visitor," the girl at the front desk said.

When I came downstairs, Joe was waiting for me where the ramp from our hallway entered the lobby. He was wearing a brand-new suede jacket.

He told me that his father, on a trip to sell clothes in Georgia, had stopped off to look for him in his room and, when he wasn't there, had found him in the library. He had offered to take him to dinner. "So I went."

"You just went? You forgot that I was there with you?"

"I didn't want him to see you and make a scene. I didn't want him to know we were there together."

"You just *abandoned* me? You snuck *away*?"

"I couldn't think of what else to do. I was worried."

"So worried you let him buy you a new jacket?"

"He bought me dinner, too."

"What did you have?"

"We went to the steak house."

"I didn't have any dinner."

"Well, let's go now, and I'll get you something to eat."

"I hate suede," I said. "Don't come near me in that jacket."

❧

That summer I decided not to go home. I didn't want to live with my parents or to see Joe during the time he was living with his. I'd had all I could take of this arrangement. I registered for summer school and got a room of my own on the fourth floor of Mallory Hall and began buying cigarettes from the machine in the student center. After my two classes, I went upstairs and smoked, one cigarette after another. I deliberately forced myself to inhale. I choked each time.

I started going out with Tim, a law student I'd met through a friend. We spent almost every evening together. He took me to movies; he cooked dinner for me in the house he shared with two other law students. Once I let him kiss me goodnight, but his breath was beery, and he felt all wrong, long and gangly where Joe was solid and strong, his body too tall for my body, where Joe's body was exactly the right size for mine. He wasn't Joe. I couldn't love him or anyone but Joe.

I walked through the heat of summer in a fog, not me, living not really my own life but an invented life, some fiction. I don't even remember what courses I took. Joe wrote me a few letters from home, called me a few times, but usually I was out. I never called him back. When he finally reached me, he told me he was going to the

93

University of Michigan in the fall. He had already gotten a room with a family. I wished him luck.

In the fall, I stayed on at Florida to complete my senior year and applied to a few graduate schools, one in California, one in Boston. I had long ago returned the engagement ring to my father. "Sell it," I told him. "Maybe someone else can enjoy it."

A few times after that, when I was home visiting my family, I spotted Joe's mother in public places, shopping on Lincoln Road or coming into a coffee shop where I was with my parents. I either ducked into a doorway so that she wouldn't see me or hid my head behind a menu. My mother still called her "Hatchet Face." I had never—before this—wanted anyone to be tortured or wished anyone dead, but I learned about hate of a violent intensity from Joe's mother. When I experienced it, the sickness I felt was more terrible than being parted from Joe.

⚭

But in the end we couldn't stay parted. Seven years from the time I had offered to play duets with Joe (but never did), we finagled our futures into the same geographic latitude, the same graduate school in Boston, where at last—with scholarships—we were able to finish our educations without our parents' assistance. In June 1960, we flew home from Boston to Miami Beach to be married. Joe's parents came to our wedding in the Crown Hotel on Collins Avenue. His mother dressed in beige satin. Joe's parents sat with mine at the newlyweds' table and drank champagne, but they never addressed me directly.

Joe and I settled in Boston for a time, where our first daughter was born, then moved to California, where we had our second and third little girls. Joe's sister was also living in California with her husband and two children. Both sets of parents moved to California, to watch their grandchildren grow up.

Joe's mother and father came regularly to visit us. We often went to their apartment for dinner. They sent birthday gifts for the girls, sizable Chanukah checks to Joe and me. When the girls were still small, Joe's father, though he was no longer a traveling salesman, made sure they had pretty clothes from the line of children's wear he had represented.

No word was ever said to me about the way I was treated.

⚜

Joe's father died at the age of seventy-seven, on Yom Kippur, after the summer our eldest girl was married (he lived to see the wedding), and Joe's mother died seven years later. We went to see her as she lay on her deathbed. She had stopped eating by then and was barely able to breathe. She said to Joe, "After I'm dead, it will all be alright." Then she called me closer to her bedside. With difficulty, she extended her hand. With difficulty, I took it and held it.

"I want you to know," she whispered, "you made a good wife for my son."

My Suicides

On April Fool's Day last year, one of my students, a twenty-three-year-old young man with a long, blond ponytail, sealed his mouth with silver duct tape, put a plastic bag over his head, and managed to make himself die.

"The self has gone away and all the atoms are seething," he wrote in his suicide note, left on his Web site along with a photo of himself shown vaguely in shadow inside a screened window, his form already fading into the ether.

"Please don't cage it in a box and weigh it down with polished granite. Cremate it. And don't save the ashes in some silly container . . . toss them on the desert . . . I want to be a cactus next!"

His Web site offered a number of personal notes to his friends and many of his poems and paintings, as well as the only story he had ever written (for my class), on the strength of which, he had told me at our conference, he wanted to quit school and become a writer.

We had sat that afternoon in my windowless office on the campus and discussed his future. He had read his story, titled "Generation X," to our class the week before. All my students were nervous about reading their stories aloud; sometimes their voices trembled or the pages in their hand shook.

My student's story was about drugs. Our class members were not surprised or even remotely disturbed by this: most of their own stories had to do with drugs and sex. His story involved a group of college friends who spend a few days hiking in the mountains and taking drugs. "Finally, the damn sun's gone. I'm trying to make my eyes as soft as I can. . . . Little blue butterfly . . . carry me back to the clover fields of my childhood . . . taste it dissolve, the universe will soon be smooth again, no prickly dried blood clogging every pore. Why did you give us this shit, Timothy Leary?" In the last line of the story, my student wrote: "He rolls over and looks up into the valley: the distant mountains are bathed in early morning gold, a white veil of fog hanging before them: the promised land. Turning to Justin and pointing through the veil, he says, with a twinkle: 'Let's go there.'"

Where, exactly, my student's hero wanted to go did not seem ominous to me until the dean phoned me one morning and told me my student was dead. He had dropped out of school and had given away many of his belongings to his friends and told them he was moving to Santa Cruz to become a writer. He had told me, when he discussed quitting school, that he wasn't worried about making a living. He could work part-time for his food. As for lodging, he still had keys to the lab, and he could always sleep there. I had told him, as I felt I must, all the reasons he should not drop out of school: "You can't count on making a living as a writer; science is a more reliable field than literature. A life devoted to art is about as certain as the lottery."

"I know all that, of course," he said to me, pulling his hand down the length of his pony tail. Had I been twenty again, I could have fallen in love with this young man, a gentle soul who wore his torment in his eyes, a physically beautiful boy—delicately graceful, blue-eyed, tall and slender. Of his farming family across the country, he said, "My parents don't know anything about me. They can't figure me out."

After our talk, he offered me his hand. His fingers were cold and damp. I wished him luck; I told him to be sure to stay in touch with me. A few days later, I passed a grassy knoll on campus and saw him stretched out, his hands behind his head, staring at the blue sky. He caught sight of me and sat up, guiltily. I smiled and nodded my appreciation, envying his youth, his poetic trance, his dreamy face turned to the sun. Not so long after, I had the phone call that told me he had killed himself and transformed his seething atoms into ashes for the cactus plants in the desert.

An informal memorial service was held for him on campus a month later. I and two of his other teachers spoke about him. A number of his friends were sprawled on the grass near the student center. His drawings and paintings had been taped to a nearby wall.

I told the students not to romanticize his death; I told them suicide was not a courageous act and in his case was a waste. I said what I had to say—but I felt that Hamlet's conundrum was at the podium with me. My student's friend stood and spoke about religion and Jesus and about how being born again had helped him to understand the meaning of life and death and how he loved the lost young man more than ever now and knew he would see him again in the presence of God. I was sorry that someone else, another science student, didn't dispute or argue this in any way.

After the service, the registrar, who was my friend, came up and told me she was glad I had taken a tough line, not showing pity or admiration for this kind of death. We shared chips and guacamole dip with the others and afterward looked at my student's paintings as if we were in an art gallery. One painting was of an enormous eagle with a beady eye who has, balanced on his rounded head, a tiny observatory. My student had clearly been making fun of man's puny attempt at "seeing" versus the deep black eye of the true seer.

⟋∞⟍

My very earliest suicide was Tante Iphiga's daughter, Bertha. She killed herself on Easter Sunday when I was eleven years old. I was sitting on the front stoop of our house in Brooklyn, watching the Christian families walk to church—especially the girls in their black patent leather Mary Janes and ruffled dresses and big straw hats with ribboons streaming down the back. I envied girls who had been lucky enough to be born to a family that celebrated Easter. Jewish families had a few big holidays, but not one was as colorful and festive as this. In my mind I was humming Bing Crosby's rendition of "In Your Easter Bonnet" when I was called inside the house and told that something serious had happened to our cousin Bertha—so serious that she was dead.

I remember trying to adopt a pained demeanor—I didn't know Bertha, and I wanted to stay outside and envy the pretty dresses of the girls in the Easter parade. (Bertha was the daughter of my grandmother's brother and his wife, who had the strange name of Tante Iphiga.) All I knew about Bertha was that she had been dropped on her head as a baby and was never quite right after that. She secretly married an Italian and continued to live at home till her mother found her wedding band in a box of her sanitary napkins. She then went to live with the Italian, who treated her badly. He didn't want children, so she began to raise pigeons on the roof of her apartment.

When I was grown up, I learned what sketchy facts the family knew of her life. The Italian husband had a violent temper. He liked to go to big family weddings and funerals. Bertha liked to stay home with her pigeons. On her last Easter Sunday, he went off without her to a wedding. She stuffed towels under the doorframes and around the windows, put the cat outside, turned on the gas, and killed herself.

As a child, I could see that this suicide caused everyone great distress. No one knew whether to feel sorry or angry, sympathetic or disgusted. They wondered whether they could have been kinder to Bertha. She had a hard life. She wasn't pretty. No one in the family ever visited her. I wished I had visited her and seen her pigeons. I was sorry she had married a cruel husband. And I was sorry she had ruined my Easter.

✳

When I had been married for twenty-two years and had three children of my own, my brother-in-law tried to make me an accomplice to his suicide. My sister was hiding with her two sons in a battered women's shelter. Their number one rule was "You may not call your batterer or abuser." Unable to reach my sister, he called me dozens of times a day, threatening to kill me and my family if I didn't tell him where my sister was, threatening to kill himself if I didn't get my sister to call him back within the next five minutes. Each time he called me, I turned on the tape recorder so that I could later play his pleas to my sister, partly to keep her informed and partly to defend myself against being the only arbiter of his fate. When he called, he pled his arguments to *me,* made his bargains with *me,* declared his love for my sister to *me,* knowing that one way or another this information would get back to her.

When I was home alone, I carried mace in my pocket. I hid the sharp knives in a hall cabinet, out of his sight but easy for me to reach in case I was forced to defend myself. I watched the street from behind my closed blinds in case he might be hiding in wait for me or my daughters. Twice he followed me in his car as I drove on my errands. He knew that sooner or later I would have to visit my sister, and then he would find her.

The police could not help me. They said a crime would have to be committed first before they could pick him up. A man sitting quietly in his car on a public street was not committing a crime. When he called and begged me to invite him to dinner, I forced myself to remember the violence he had already done at his home, pounding his head through a wall in anger, biting his baby son on the scalp like an enraged animal. He had pulled a table to pieces, he had thrown a toilet seat at my sister because she wouldn't agree to sell the house so that he could buy options on gold futures. When the price of gold went up and he blamed her for losing their fortune, he threatened her life, reasoning that death could not be worse than what they were already going through.

And I, in my quiet home, with my children and my good husband, in my measured and reasoned life, became an accomplice to his fury, to his grief—and I was filled with fear.

One Saturday night, while my husband and daughters and I were having dinner, he called and said that if I didn't get my sister on the phone to him in the next ten minutes, he would be dead. This time, he said, he meant it. He knew just how to do it, and he was going to do it. I begged him not to, told him that things would work out, that if only he would agree to have counseling, medication, he could come out of this—but just then my husband came up behind me and took the phone out of my hands. "Don't bother us anymore," he said. "Don't call here anymore. If you want to kill yourself, then just do it. But don't bother us." He hung up.

My children stared at him as if he had pulled the trigger himself. I began to shiver. I called my sister at the shelter and told her what her husband had said. She was sick then, with high fever. Her voice was as hoarse and deep as a man's. *I'll call him,* she said. *I'll tell him I love him. Because I do.*

Five minutes later she called me back to say that no one had answered the phone at the house. She said she was too sick to care. She said she was going to go back to bed and cover her face with a blanket.

On Monday morning, I went shopping for food. No one had heard from my brother-in-law since the call on Saturday night. With my groceries in the car, I was driving across a street that went over a wash, a long corridor coming down from the mountains in which rainwater ran to the sea. In the wash I saw a family of peacocks. A peahen, dun-colored, drab, and her two chicks were walking slowly in the shallow rivulets of water and matted leaves. They seemed lost and confused. They walked first to one side of the wash, then the other. It was hard to imagine how they had got in there, or how they would get out. But my eyes were searching in vain for the peacock, the male with his bright colored fan of feathers, his shimmering energy, his beauty. He was not there.

When I got home, I was carrying bags of food in from the car when the phone rang. My brother-in-law's sister told me that police had found him dead in his car, parked in a far corner of the top level of a parking garage, the hose of the vacuum cleaner attached to the exhaust pipe and coming in the rear window. He had been dead probably since Saturday. At the house, police found his insurance policy, flung on the floor just inside the door of the living room so that my sister would find it there, his final message of fury and revenge.

⚯

The fourth of my suicides was a woman my own age, a well-known author of teenage novels, a woman who—as they always say of people who seem to have it all—"had everything to live for." She had a successful career, a devoted husband, and two beautiful children. Her record of publications and sales would be the envy of any writer. She lived in a fine apartment in New York City, and she wrote a new book every year from October 1 to October 31. Her rule for herself, which she told me about, was this: "You must write ten pages a day, or you will be shot." I admired her industry. She chose October in which to write her novel because it was a bleak month. Her children were in school, there was no sun in the sky, she wrote all morning every morning and every afternoon went to a movie by herself. The books she wrote each October were her young adult novels; later in the year she would also write a novel for adults. Once a book was finished, there was the excitement of selling it, usually for a good deal of money. She was brave in treating subjects for young people—unmarried sex (a divorced parent having a love affair), a mixed-race romance, a boy who chooses to raise the baby his pregnant girlfriend wants to abort—and late in her career she wrote of euthanasia, the killing of an ailing grandparent by the heroine's father, out of mercy. My friend's books were often removed from library shelves; she fought against censorship and traveled to speak out against it. We began writing to each other after our mutual agent died and we were both seeking a new agent. She gave me advice, personal and professional. She held back no secrets—she talked about money the way adults usually don't, telling me about the exact amount of her own earnings, about her husband's, about the advances she knew had been given to other writers. She spoke of secrets, hers, her husband's, and her children's. Without guilt, she read their diaries and letters. I was not so candid; I had a sense of boundaries that she did not seem to have, which was also why I wrote with relative caution and she wrote so freely and bluntly. Once, when she came to visit me, I picked her up at the airport. On the way to my house, she began telling me the plot of a novel she planned to begin in October. As she talked with obvious excitement, we passed a burning house. Fire trucks were arriving, their sirens blasting. Smoke was pouring from the windows of the house, and people were gathered across the street to watch. My friend didn't even seem to notice the spectacle; her mind was somewhere else, her brain filled with the images of her book-to-be, her fantasies stronger than the burning reality at hand. During our visit, we talked for three days, stopping only to eat and sleep briefly. But mainly she talked and I listened. She was bursting with talk; her head was under enormous pressure from her visions and her ideas. Her daughters, like mine, were adolescent girls. We spoke about their new sexuality, how we dealt with it, what we feared from it. And she told me she had taken her daughters to see a pornographic movie—that they might as well be exposed to such films in her presence as be shocked by them later, without her there to explain things. I was the one shocked—I was frightened that she wanted to control their minds to that extent, that she felt it was her duty to initiate them personally into aspects of life that were not her business.

When I visited her in New York, she gave me a blanket for my bed made out of the ties of her dead father, who had been a psychoanalyst. She told me she was his angel of perfection—that she could do no wrong in his eyes. She confessed that, after he died, she had tried to kill herself, but had failed. She said it perkily, as if that had been just a mistake, over and done with. One wall of her library was filled with the books of Virginia Woolf, who was her heroine and inspiration. She told me that any woman who came after Woolf and wrote a book was already defeated: Virginia Woolf had done the best that could ever be done—and died with stones in her pocket in the River Ouse at the age of fifty-nine.

We wrote letters to each other for fifteen years. Hers were single-spaced, four or more pages long, answered the minute she received mine, as I answered hers. What we had was a fevered long-distance conversation, two women typing madly at opposite ends of the country, consoling each other's literary disappointments, encouraging each other's ideas and plans.

In the library, one day, I read a devastating review of my friend's newest adult novel, a book about a woman who had been in a mental hospital for a year, and I was astonished by the casual cruelty of the review, the way the reviewer had tossed out bombs of viciousness. A few days later, at lunchtime (I was frying kosher hot dogs in a pan; their grease was sizzling and spattering burning droplets on my hands), the phone rang and a woman whose voice I had never heard told me she was a friend of my friend and had some bad news for me.

"When did she kill herself?" I cried out, and the woman, who was prepared only to tell me my friend had been sick and died (the newspapers said, a few days later, that her death was caused by "septic poisoning"), had to concede that she had "taken something" and had been on a respirator for ten days before she died. I berated myself. I should have known something was wrong because no letter had come for more than a week. And, like all survivors of suicide, in the afterknowledge of the death, I knew I hadn't called early enough or soon enough . . . hadn't really cared enough or been alert enough.

"She was only fifty," the woman told me. Perhaps, like Virginia Woolf, my friend had chosen to escape her torment and bypass old age.

When I flew to New York for the funeral, I stayed with my friend's mother, a woman in her eighties who lived in a huge apartment near Central Park. The walls were filled with clippings of my friend's reviews, photos of her, framed awards, and snapshots of her two daughters. Together, her old mother and I took a bus to the church, where a gathering of writers and editors sang praises to my dead friend. Her husband told me afterward that she had called him at work and told him she'd "done something." He had asked her if she had taken pills (he admitted to me he had been hiding her pills for the last few months). He had assured her he was calling paramedics and would be right home. He later learned from the paramedics that, when they arrived at her door, she had opened it and told them there must be some mistake; it wasn't her, look at her, she was just fine. And so they had left. Her husband had been caught in traffic in Central Park. My friend had actually gone down to the lobby to get her mail (writers must always get their mail) before she collapsed. By the time her husband arrived home and called the paramedics a second time, she was comatose. Her family buried her at the edge of a river, with a stone on which was engraved "Beauty mysteriously unfolding."

∽

My mother's sister, an old woman, didn't quite achieve her suicide but left enough bloody fingerprints on the phone, enough blood on the sink beside the double-edged razor blade, and pools of it in the bed and on the floor, to convince me it was a real act and not, as her psychiatrist told me later, just a "cry for help." However, my aunt did call me half an hour after she slit both her wrists and the vein in the crook of one elbow to ask me where she should hide her diamond ring: she didn't want the "crooks here to get it." When I first picked up the phone, her voice was low: "Merrill, I'm tired of living," she said. I said, as I did every day, sympathetically, "I know. I understand how much you miss Uncle Moe, but there's nothing you can do about it but wait and hope your feelings will improve," and she said "There is something I can do. I already did it." "You did what?" "I slit my wrists. Don't call anyone."

I stopped to think hard. I actually considered doing as she asked. I had watched my uncle die of lung cancer. I had seen the colored pen marks on his chest where the radiation was aimed, seen him unable to swallow because of his charred esophagus, seen the purple bleeding holes on his ankles, seen him gasping for breath under the oxygen mask in the hospital. I had also visited her a hundred times since her widowhood, sat with my aunt on her living room couch in the retirement home with the other old crones, smelled their smell as we all crowded into the small elevator to go down for the watered soup and canned peas for lunch. Why call for help and bring her back to that and the rest of it—her own decay, her inevitable stroke, her broken hip, her feeding tube (all of which I'd witnessed with my mother). These thoughts passed through my mind as I held the phone, and then I saw my husband walk by the doorway of my office, and I blurted out: "It's my aunt; she's slit her wrists and doesn't want me to call paramedics."

"You have to," he said simply.

So I called the paramedics. My action was responsible for her ambulance ride, her ten-day lockup in the mental ward of the hospital, the counseling with other crazies, a roommate who peed on the floor of their room at 2:00 A.M. During that period, I had to go to her retirement home and clean up the blood, asking myself every second (as I threw away all her scissors, knives, pins, razor blades, and screwdrivers) whether I should have let her bleed to death and be done with it. Now we were all in for it—more old age, more grief, and death anyway.

We moved her to another retirement home, and she went on living and regretting that she hadn't done a better job with the razor blade.

A long time ago, I took a job on a suicide hotline after six weeks of training. The office was in a double-locked room in an unused wing of a small local hospital. The room was tiny—one chair, a desk, a phone, a teapot, a few paperback novels. Someone had taped up a list of specific instructions to tell the callers: Make yourself a peanut butter sandwich. Put on a sweater. Promise me you'll do what I'm telling you, and call me back in fifteen minutes when you are calmer and tell me exactly where you live. We can help you. I swear you won't always feel this way.

Each time the phone rang, I felt a shiver, and the hairs on my arms stood up. "My husband knocked out my two teeth and won't let me get them fixed. He doesn't want me smiling at other men. He won't let me out of the house. I found his gun. I'm going to use it."

"Make yourself a peanut butter sandwich," I would say. "Tell me your address."

"I'm a sixty-year-old man with stomach cancer. I weigh eighty-four pounds. I'm in terrible pain, and I have no family. I know a place where I can jump off the roof."

"Put on a sweater," I would say. "Pour yourself a glass of milk, and promise you'll call me back and give me your address."

Usually they never called back. I scanned the newspapers the next day to see whether anyone had jumped off a roof or shot herself. If I did get someone to confess his address, I would have the emergency team sent out. I wasn't allowed to ask the outcome of their rescue.

Often, in that little locked room, I got obscene phone calls. The same man called night after night. I began to welcome his calls, sensing the man's obvious enjoyment of life. "I'm picturing you without clothes. I'm doing it right now as I talk to you, honey. Unbutton your blouse for me."

"Do it all you want," I would say, "as long as you don't kill yourself. Call me back when you're done, and I'll refer you to a place that can help you."

After my brother-in-law's suicide, I accompanied my sister to a meeting of Survivors-of-Suicide. We met in a shabby building in the city's downtown area and sat on torn vinyl chairs, eating packaged cookies and holding cups of tea. Everyone told his story, the parents of the teenage boy who had hung himself, the daughter of the old man who, standing in the woods behind his house, had shot himself in the mouth, the brother of the girl who had put poison in her coffee and then left a sign on the stairwell saying "Beware if you enter. Danger! Cyanide inside."

The facilitator told us to try to see our guilt for what it was, helplessness in the face of an unimaginable mystery, and to absolve ourselves: "We who choose to live can never really understand why the person we love chose to die."

We all were asked to describe the thoughts that haunted us. Each person described his special memory: the knock of the police at the door, the endless ringing of a phone when the loved one should have picked it up, the baffling suicide note, the image of the locked car in the garage with a person slumped in the seat. My sister described the sight of the presents her husband had wrapped and left for her on the kitchen counter before he fled the house to kill himself.

I, who was just a visitor there, declined to take my place with the other family members to describe my recollections. Though my suicides lived in me, I did not belong in this first rank of loss. Privately, I saw my brother-in-law on my doorstep, begging to be let in. I saw him alone in his cold and dark house without his family, frantically calling me. But what I thought of most often was the sight of the puzzled peacocks, the peahen and her lost chicks, in the high-walled wash that wove its way downhill under the city streets and under the homes of happy families and to the sea.

The Harpsichord on the Mountain

Because my husband had some years earlier taught in Florence for his university, we decided to return and live there *senza gli studenti* for a month to see the city on our own. My husband, who was a lover of early music and had built his own harpsichord many years before, had been urged by his musical friends to look up a famous American harpsichordist who lived in Florence. The man was known to have several rare historical instruments; he had been cordial to other amateur players from the United States who had visited him there. We took his phone number with us, but I knew it would take time for my husband to get up the courage to call him. He could not be rushed in such matters.

As soon as we were settled in our apartment, though, we did visit the workshop of a restorer of old instruments. She was a gracious woman who welcomed us into one of those crumbling street-front doorways and led us through passageways of ancient stone till the hallway opened out into a brightly lit workshop, where two other women were bent over harpsichords and pianofortes. Adjoining the workshop was a small but elegant concert hall whose walls were covered with likenesses of Bach. The owner gladly showed us her instruments in progress, and she, too, urged my husband to call the famous harpsichordist who lived near the Porta Romana.

We had many other things we wanted to do in Florence. My husband knew more Italian than I did, but I could manage the basics— shopping for food *("Quattro piatte prosciutto cotto, per favore")* and clothing *("Posso avere un po' di sconto?")*. With the help of a friend who knew an agent, we had rented two rooms in the Palazzo Pucci, a five-hundred-year-old apartment house on Via Ricasoli in *il centro* of Florence. If I looked out our third-floor living room window to the left, I could see the bell tower of the Duomo two blocks away. To the right was the Accademia, where Michelangelo's *David* was perched on a pedestal so high that, in order to see his face, one had to focus first upon his genitals and then look upward.

The day we visited the Accademia, a girl fainted from the apparently unbearable beauty of the statue above her. A chair was brought for her, and her companion, a much older man, stood behind her chair and from time to time patted her face. Each time she opened her eyes and raised them to David's face, she'd swoon again, her eyes rolling up into her head. Her companion continued to hold her face between his hands. For a moment I had a desire to swoon against my husband and have him bring me to. I'd read about this fainting syndrome, common in Florence—caused by an excess of art and beauty—but I'd never experienced it. If I stayed too long in a museum, I would get hungry and begin to imagine an Italian pizza, uncut on a plate, thin crusted, perhaps *"quattro stagioni"* or *"prosciutto e funghi,"* and art would flee from my mind.

Though we'd been jubilant at the location of our rooms, we'd forgotten that any apartment overlooking a street in the center of Florence would constantly be filled with the deafening buzz and roar of *motorini*. At certain hours, the noise of the scooters reached such levels that my husband and I could not speak to one another without shouting.

"How do Italians stand it?" I screamed to him. He was sitting in the enormous living room about three inches from the television, trying to improve his Italian by listening to a quiz show. He didn't hear me. He had a blanket over his head. It was nearly the end of October, and the weather was turning cold. Italians did not use heat in their homes till the first of November, unless an emergency weather situation called forth a decree from the government. I was sitting at an antique desk wearing sweater and coat. I was trying to type on my computer, but my fingers were too chilled to move accurately over the keys. I didn't know yet whether I was enjoying myself in Italy, though, when I sent e-mails home, I thought it sounded impressive to write our grown children, "We are living in a palace with seventeenth-century oil paintings of the Pucci family hanging on the walls. Antiques are in every cabinet. The Marchesa Pucci has an office downstairs from which she controls the family empire: textiles, wine, and clothing designed by Emilio Pucci (her famous and dead husband). The shop right next to this building sells Pucci clothing—I priced a handkerchief with a Pucci design, it cost $65. God forbid we should spill wine on our Pucci tablecloth; we have signed away our lives to leave everything exactly as we found it."

Pucci, Gucci, I really didn't know one from the other. At home I shopped in thrift shops, which was a form of entertainment to me. I liked to browse through the items among which other people had lived (and died). I was not impressed by designer clothes and in fact had a low opinion of the elegant, aristocratic Emilio Pucci, who, from what I'd read, had been in love with himself and had spent too much time away from his young wife having dalliances with other women. From a book I'd read about him at home I had photocopied certain pages in the hope that one day I could have a chat with the *Marchesa* and show her pictures of herself at her wedding, of herself standing on the roof of this very building (with the great Duomo in the background) in the blush of her first love. One photo showed Emilio Pucci mounted on a black steed, in a black velvet cape and black boots, about to lead off the pageant of "*calcio* in costume," as imposing and threatening as Mozart's *Commendatore.*

The marchesa, now a woman of about sixty, was guarded by two employees—one a bulldog-faced matron, the other an eighteen-year-old beauty named Sabrina, with blond hair falling in delicate tendrils about her Botticellian face. These women worked in an office on the first floor of our building. The marchesa worked in another office opposite theirs. I knew that, at the sound of the *ascensore* descending from the floors above (those freezing rooms that the marchesa rented to Americans for astronomical prices), Sabrina and the bulldog woman would rush into the hall to prevent anyone from attempting to walk into the garden at the rear of the house and thus to pass the open door of the marchesa's office. We lived in fact in a fortress, the front door so thick and heavy I had to turn the key and push with my shoulder to enter the inner chamber, which was itself like an empty, dimly lit prison cell. To get beyond it, through the floor-to-ceiling bars and to the elevator, I needed a second key. A third key opened our apartment door.

Sabrina, who handled the tenants, knew almost no English, so we made much use of pantomime. I tried to tell her that the pots in our tiny kitchen had no covers. Since all the pots (dented and nearly useless) had metal handles, I needed a pot holder. And since each room had only one electrical outlet, I also needed an extension cord—otherwise it was impossible to turn on the living room light, the TV, and my laptop computer at once. The beautiful girl nodded her head and smiled and indicated that all would be taken care of. I had no sense that she understood anything I'd said, and, when I found a light bulb at my door the next day, I was certain.

Our apartment had one huge living room, one small bedroom, one tiny kitchen, and one infinitesimal bathroom, which was at the far end of the living room and seemed to have been carved out of the huge blocks of stone that made up the building. The shower enclosure was of cracked and peeling plaster, but the shower handles were gold. There was no shower door or curtain, so water sprayed all over the floor and walls. The towels were always damp and smelled of mildew. There was no way to get them dry—no clothesline to hang them on, no heated radiators to drape them over. The apartment generally smelled like a dirty dishrag.

I entertained myself much of the time by leaning out the window that opened on Via Ricasoli. Across the street, in the third-floor rooms of the opposite building, I could see young women working at computers. On the floor below, I always saw the same dark-haired woman sweeping the floors or washing her windows. On the narrow, canyonlike street, people flew by on scooters. Women on their way to work wore dress suits and heels and kept their leather purses protected on the floorboards between their feet. Young men in black leather jackets and helmets tore down the street on motors that never knew a muffler. A shop across the street, called "Vice Versa," displayed a windowful of brightly colored plastic kitchenware, splashes of orange and yellow and green in the drab, stone-colored street. Often people clustered at the shop window, jostling one another, on rainy days tangling their umbrellas. They seemed fascinated by the neon-bright juice pitchers, the translucent cutting boards, the American-sized coffee mugs, the see-through cutlery. A block away was Michelangelo's *David,* but the Italians craved plastic dinnerware. When I went into the store myself one day, I was shocked at the prices. At home I could buy a plastic pitcher for a dollar in the 99 Cent Store; in Italy such an item was 40,000 lire, about $28.

I worried about how much money we were spending. Each time I sent an e-mail on my computer, the *scatti* ticked by (a counter measured how many minutes I used the phone). Someone had told me that if I used the phone before 6:30 a.m., the charges would be much cheaper. I'd often get up at dawn, run through the freezing living room with a blanket wrapped around my shoulders, sit down at the antique desk, and log on to my e-mail server. I'd write my daughters the news of the day:

Yesterday evening we had ossobuco for dinner, and, later, as we walked across the Arno, we saw a mime on the Ponte Vecchio. He was robed in a Roman toga, spraypainted silver, and he stood as still as a statue for perhaps fifteen minutes while people came up and dropped coins in the silver bowl at his feet. Then, very slowly, he'd raise his arm, as one waking from the dead, to thank those who made contributions. On our way home, we stopped at a profumeria, where Daddy bought me earplugs. When the girl brought out foam rubber plugs, Daddy asked her if they didn't have something more "forte" (he indicated the "motos" going by)—and she found us a box of pink wax earplugs. We paid $9 for them! I hope they work tonight. Our bed has two blankets on it—one made of wool with a Pucci label on it, and one that seems to be an animal skin of some kind, heavy as lead, with fur on one side, smooth like leather on the other. It smells a hundred years old. A cabinet beside our bed, made of wood, has a pull-out drawer with a chamber pot in it! We are living here in the middle ages. Yesterday I hoped to meet the marchesa and brought down some pages I'd photocopied from a book about her. She heard me ask her assistant whether I might give them to her and slammed her office door against me. She is clearly not interested in Italian-American relations. I have heard that her life is very sad, that she lost a son in a car accident, and that her heart was broken by the womanizing of her famous husband. I am so lucky to have married Daddy. He can be found every night in front of the TV with a blanket over his head, so I always know where he is.

❧

As a personal protest against the prices in the Pucci shop next door, I took the bus to the outskirts of Florence, where we had once lived and where I'd often visited a little *mercato usato*—a thrift shop. A woman was just locking up the shop for the day. I recognized her and called out, "Paola!" In a moment she was embracing me, her face alight with welcome. She unlocked the door and invited me in, even though the sign on the shop said *"Chiuso."* Inside, the tiny store was crammed with clothing of every sort, some items hanging up high, some folded in little cubbyholes, some piled in plastic baskets and labeled *Donna, Uomo, Pantaloni, Camicie, Vestiti.* Winter coats were 10,000 lire ($7). Everything else was a dollar or two. But on this day Paola pointed out to me an iridescent blouse hanging in the window, a garment made of a glowing purple knit shot through with silver threads. She took the blouse off the hanger and held it up. The label read "Gucci." The real thing! *"Aah, bella."* She handed it to me. *"Un regalo."* A gift, for coming to see her. We hugged once more. She stuffed into a bag other presents, as well: a silk scarf, a leather belt, a sweater with enormous flowers embroidered on it, a battery-run radio/alarm clock whose directions, in Italian, I would never decipher. We embraced a final time when I left. I smiled to myself all the way home. I was certain that today I loved Italy. But when the bus-control police boarded the bus, locked the doors, and demanded to see everyone's ticket in order to catch anyone who was trying to ride free, then I hated Italy.

I returned to the Pucci Palace with my Gucci blouse. That night my husband and I walked to the piazza in front of the Duomo, where I bought a piece of jewelry from an Indian tradesman who had set up a stand with bits of glass and tin resembling jewelry. I chose a mother-of-pearl (plastic) dolphin on a silver (tin) chain for $3. It matched beautifully the silver threads in the Gucci blouse.

After we had dinner of pesto and wine at one of the trattorias beyond the piazza, we walked to the Lutheran church on the other side of the river to hear a Bach organ concert. We had been on the lookout for harpsichord concerts; one was advertised on fliers announcing a medieval costume drama, handed out on the Ponte Vecchio by young women dressed in red velvet gowns. But my husband thought the price was too high for a performance that was unlikely to feature authentic historical instruments.

Only a few people were attending the organ concert. At the first chords of Bach, I felt the music coming up and into my body through the wooden pews. There was nothing on the walls of the church, no bleeding Christ, no saints under glass, not one gold-leaf pulpit or *pietà* or burning rank of candles. We heard only Bach's godly music singing through the thundering pipes. The organist sat at a keyboard high above the pews, his back to the backs of the audience. He played as if he were bodiless, or at least as if the body he inhabited were of no consequence to him. When he had played the final notes, he took no bows and gave no encores. He disappeared and left only the vibrations reverberating in our bones.

The night was cold when we got out; it had rained. We crossed the Arno and paused to watch the streetlights ride over the ripples of the current. A couple was kissing a few feet away. Lovers were kissing all over Florence. I had taken a whole roll of film of nothing but lovers kissing—at bus stops, over plates of pasta, outside the *rosticceria,* inside the *gelateria.* I sometimes wished my husband would have an impulse to kiss me in a public place, but I'd known him since I was fifteen. He wasn't likely to satisfy such a fantasy.

❧

I had a sense, as we approached our doorway on Via Ricasoli, that a man was following us, but not on the narrow sidewalk. He was walking slightly behind us in the middle of the street. When we got to our doorway, I put my key in the lock, and at that moment the man darted between the scooters parked on the street and rang the lowest doorbell on the wall just beside me. The streetlight reflected off his black leather pants. He stood, breathing hard, right behind me. I knew at once he didn't belong there, that the bell he pressed rang only in the marchesa's office on the first floor, and that neither she nor her workers were ever there at night. This man, I understood in a flash, was going to enter the building as we did and trap us between the locked front door and the locked iron gate beyond it. Either that, or he would follow us into the elevator and rob us upstairs—or worse. I knew my husband had no inkling of this. He was born without a sense of danger; his mind did not contain the normal cautionary apparatus. I astonished him by pulling my key out of the lock, grabbing his arm, and saying loudly, "Let's go and buy a gelato." I dragged him along the street in the direction of the Accademia, beyond which was a popular gelateria.

"What?" he said. "Now? So late?" But I was glancing over my shoulder, watching the man rush away from our door in the other direction. We had narrowly missed having something terrible happen to us, and I was shaking at the thought of our hair-thin escape. I didn't want to eat ice cream, but I insisted we each buy a gelato. I wanted time to be sure the man was gone, time to gather my senses in the brightly lit shop that always had people in it. *Nocciola*—hazelnut—was the flavor I preferred, but I couldn't even taste it. I was already shivering, and the gelato made me colder. When I told my husband what I had thought was going to happen, and how we probably had barely escaped being mugged or killed, he was doubtful. I explained why I had to be right about this: the late night, the fact that we were obviously tourists, what I'd heard about drug users and their need for money, how the man couldn't have been visiting anyone in the building at that hour, that the buzzer he rang did not belong to one of the rented apartments, how he had run away when we hadn't entered the building. My husband didn't contradict me, but I knew he didn't believe that our lives had been in danger. His skepticism and stubborn lack of fear made him seem dense. The thought that I had married a dense human being frightened me.

In the Milan train station, we'd nearly been killed because he refused to hail a cab when I asked him to. En route to Florence, we'd flown from Los Angeles to Malpensa Airport and had stayed the night in a Milan hotel that advertised its location as "right across the street from the station." Our plan was to take the train to Florence in the morning.

However, we had four suitcases between us, and the "street" was enormous, with many roadways converging from many angles upon the train station. I argued that we should call a cab. My husband felt we could easily pull our suitcases on wheels, one in each hand, across the many intersections. He didn't like to call cabs if he could walk or take a bus. I knew he felt helpless in a cab, at the mercy of the driver who, in some way, had us in his power.

Years before, also in Milan, we had mistakenly parked our rented car in a tow-away zone near a museum. When we came out, our car, with all our luggage (and traveler's checks), was gone. A cab driver in a café overheard us calling the police and offered to drive us to the arena where cars were towed and held until a fine had been paid. When we got there, we saw hundreds of cars in rows waiting to be claimed. The cab driver proposed to take care of paying the fine, to spare us the complications and paperwork. He said the fine would be $150. My husband hesitated. "Let him do it," I whispered. "Give him the money; he understands the system here." But my husband ignored me and told the man he would pay the fine himself. The driver promptly jumped in his cab and sped away without collecting his fare. It took two hours to find our car, but the fine turned out to be $15.

When I asked our Milan hotel clerk whether a cab could get us close to the trains, he said, yes, a cab would take us around the back of the station and to the level of the tracks. My husband still wanted to cross the street by foot. We staggered like drunken sailors toward the station, each of us jerking and hauling the heavy suitcases up and down curbs, pulling, pushing, or pulling and pushing simultaneously, threatened by speeding cars, our arm sockets nearly torn out by the time we gained the safety of the sidewalk. What presented itself to us then was a new obstacle: a long flight of steps ascending to the entrance to the station. The words sat on my tongue like a frog: *If we'd taken a cab.* . . . But I didn't say them, since I had the sense to remember where this kind of conversation would lead. We both needed our strength.

My husband told me to stay below and took one suitcase at a time to the top of the staircase, until three were lined up at the top. For a moment I felt he was chivalrous, and my heart softened. He looked quite handsome in his raincoat and turtleneck shirt, his hair blowing wildly in the chilly air. Then he took the fourth suitcase in one hand and my hand in his other and helped me up the stairs. In the lobby of the station, we saw that there was yet another level to reach—this time by escalator. Others already on the escalator were transporting their luggage upward in wire carts on wheels. My husband spotted the source of these carts and, leaving me guarding the suitcases, was away for so long that I feared we would miss our train. By the time he came back pushing two carts, I was cursing my luggage, all the shoes and sweaters and dresses so carefully chosen with an image of myself in Italy "appropriately dressed for all occasions." I realized it didn't matter what either of us wore; we weren't being judged for our good fashion sense, and the stuff was killing us. I could hardly breathe from pushing my tons of junk around.

We somehow got two suitcases balanced on each wire cart. I tried to push mine forward, but it stopped short and the handle crashed into my breasts. My husband showed me that, in order to make the cart move, I had to press upward on a wire bar under the handle. We soon understood the reason. Once a cart was pushed onto the escalator, with two wheels on one step and two on a lower step, the wheels locked for safety until the bar was pressed to move the cart forward.

We were moving upward when I looked up to see where the ride would end. The level on which we would board our train was a vast distance above us. We had a long moment to rest before gaining the top.

I was looking down at the station floor below when suddenly something happened. The woman ahead of my husband reached the top of the escalator and couldn't move her wagon off the moving staircase. The stairs disappeared from under her and threw her back against my husband's wagon. He couldn't move forward and fell back against my wagon, pushing me back against the person behind me. I screamed and felt myself falling down the escalator. I heard the astonished cries and curses of others, who also began tumbling downward. I had a sense we were all falling into hell from a height as great as that of the ceiling of the Sistine Chapel.

I never knew whether the woman at the top found the way to release the brake from her wagon and push it forward or whether someone pulled her forcibly off the escalator—but the jam was somehow relieved, and my husband was able to get his wagon onto solid land. Whoever pushed me upward to a standing position also shoved me and my wagon off the escalator. I was faintly aware of the desperate rush of bodies to escape the folding steps; people seemed to be running to save their lives and to catch their trains.

The train to Florence stalled on the track for two hours some-where en route. We sat facing an older couple who ate salami slices and talked incessantly. I tried to position my feet between theirs under the narrow table between us. Next to my husband was a girl with a cell phone. She chattered away throughout the trip, laughing even while the train was stalled and while we all sweated in the sti-fling air. A woman in an official uniform distributed two dry biscuits wrapped in plastic to each person, and at some point the conductor passed out certificates entitling us to a partial refund of our fare, to be claimed at the Florence station.

⚬❈⚬

Toward the end of our stay in Italy, I said to my husband, "Call the harpsichord man. We don't have many days left here. Don't miss this opportunity." I urged him each day, and then one afternoon I saw him at the little desk where the phone and my computer sat. "Yes," I heard him say, "I'm a harpsichord player, just an amateur, but a player. Yes, my wife and I would very much like to do that. Yes. Do you know what bus would take us to Porta Romana? We live near the center. I see. Yes, a cab. But what about a bus? The number 12? Yes, I see. Thank you. We'll be there between 7:30 and 8:00 tonight then. Very good."

I decided to wear my Gucci blouse and my dolphin necklace.

The harpsichordist had told my husband we could either take a cab from the Duomo, for about 20,000 lire, or take the bus at San Marco to Porta Romana. "Let's take the cab," I said.

"Let's take the bus. Then we can look around the neighborhood. And, after we see him, we can have dinner in the piazza near Porta Romana. The bus is better."

The piazza of the Porta Romana had, in its center, an enormous statue of a woman carrying what resembled a marble beam—also in the shape of a woman—on her head. The beam-like woman ex-tended far beyond the head of the woman under her, unbalancing the sculpture and giving me a sense of pain, as if I wanted to unburden her and let her rest. The whole image was distressing to look at.

"We have to find a street off to the right," my husband said, consulting his map, "and then we have to find *numero novantanove*."

"*Novantanove?*"

"Ninety-nine."

The road began to climb directly from the piazza, a steep road going straight up. We passed *numero* 1, and then walked upward for a good distance and passed *numero* 3. I was already out of breath. Ten minutes later we passed *numero* 4.

I said to my husband, "We want *numero 99*?"

"It can't be too far," he replied.

I climbed, conserving breath. Darkness was falling fast. We walked another full block to *numero* 6. At this rate, I realized, we'd have to reach the very top of the mountain to find the harpsichordist's house. Then it struck me that of course he would live on a mountaintop. He was famous. He was living in Italy. He would not have his home in the crowded apartments near the busy and noisy piazza.

The street had narrowed, and on both sides were tall stone walls. The houses hidden behind them were very far apart and marked only by solid wooden gates. Night was upon us, and cars were speeding past us up the mountain with their headlights on.

"Stand back," I yelled to my husband. "They don't expect anyone to be walking here. They probably can't even see us!"

It was not possible to walk pressed against the wall, since a culvert or ditch ran along the side of the road. We could no longer walk side by side, so my husband stepped ahead of me and took my hand to pull me along. My heart was pounding. My knees were aching with each step along the increasingly steep upward slant of the road. *This is a terrible mistake,* I wanted to say. *We should turn around and go back to the Porta Romana and get a cab.*

We were now only at number 18; then, ten minutes later, number 20. We should have been at our appointment a half hour before. It would take us (I guessed) an hour to walk back to the piazza to find a cab. By then the famous man would have assumed we weren't coming. Or by then we'd be lying dead in the road, run over like two stray dogs. My hip was beginning to pain me, and, even though I was wearing a jacket, I was beginning to shiver.

"Watch out!" I screamed as a car passed by me so closely that its side mirror grazed my body. "My God! We're going to be killed! No one expects people to be on this road. I'm sure *no one ever walks here.*"

"People walk here all the time," my husband said, though there was no one here, no one but us. I thought about this strange man I was with, about my pledge to cherish and honor him, and about the mystery of marriage.

"We're not even a third of the way there!"

"Look up ahead, I think it flattens out," he called back. "I think I see a square up there. Then many numbers will be all there in a cluster."

And the road did flatten out. I saw a little red mailbox. I imagined there would be a public phone from which we'd call a cab, maybe a café where we could rest, warm up, drink some coffee. The numbers would, like a prayer answered, leap from 22 to 99, and we would be there at the harpsichord on the mountain. All would end well.

But there was no square there, no cluster of homes, no phone. Just a mailbox at a curve in the road, and we were back climbing endlessly upward.

"Probably it's just a little further," my husband said. I hated the way his legs moved forward, toward those harpsichords he wanted so much to see, on this errand that drove everything else from his mind.

"I want to go down the mountain now," I told him. "We're nowhere near his house. We'll never find it. We're *nowhere* near it. *Do you understand that?* He won't be there even if we ever get there." I could see a few distant lights dotting their way up the mountain. No clusters, no inviting places for human beings. "If you don't turn around and come with me, I'll go down myself, without you!" I threatened. But, when I thought of going down that steep hill in the dark, alone, past the whizzing cars, I wanted to cry.

"It can't be far," my husband said. I stopped and tugged on his hand to make him face me. "Listen! That man is crazy!" I screamed.

"He was crazy not to tell you the bus doesn't go to number 99! He should have said a cab is the only way to get there!" Hysteria had taken over, and some kind of witch was working my lips. "You were too cheap to take a cab, and look where you've got us! We're going to die here! Be killed! Or freeze to death! You want me to die just so you can see those fucking harpsichords!"

My husband stopped short and faced me. I could see his expression in the glow of approaching headlights. His fists were clenched, and he was baring his teeth at me. He looked insane. Suddenly he stamped his feet.

"Just come on," he said. "Just keep going. It's the only thing to do."

He took my hand tightly and pulled me forward. I looked longingly at the stone walls, imagining that at the next gate, number 30 or 40 or 50, I would bang on the knocker till someone let me inside, let me sit down and rest, let me get warm. I stepped into the culvert and walked close to the wall. I heard dogs howling. My husband's mother had been right when she'd told him thirty-odd years ago that I wasn't the right girl for him. I wished he had listened. I tripped on something and went down on my knees.

"Give it up!" I shouted at my husband. "Just give it up!" But this time he wouldn't argue. He just tugged me to my feet and dragged me along, like baggage, like those suitcases he had jerked over the road and up the escalator at the Milan train station.

Suddenly there was no wall at the side of the road, no dogs barking, no culvert, and no cars, nothing but a cessation of signs of life. Ahead lay nothing but open field, huge, blank, empty countryside and forest beyond.

"That's it," I said. "We're at the end of the world. There are no more houses." A cold wind blew from the woods, hitting our faces. My husband finally seemed baffled. "We'll die here," I told him.

We could both see that if we moved forward we'd move into total blackness, into wilderness. There were no more cars. It was quiet, but for the wind.

"If another car passes," I said, "I'm going to stop it."

"Don't do that," my husband said. But I saw headlights coming up the hill, and I was already doing it. I stepped into the center of the road and waved my arms like a maniac. I saw myself in the headlights, a crazy woman in a Gucci blouse dancing on the road. An old red truck swerved to pass me, then slowed. I ran toward it. "I'm going with him," I screamed over my shoulder to my husband, "no matter where he's going."

My husband ran after me. A young man got out of the truck. I began to babble, "We are lost, we are lost!" but the man, who looked sympathetic, didn't understand me. *"Novantanove,"* I cried. "There is no such number, but *mio marito*" — (now I found words) — *"mio marito é non logico!"* I grabbed my husband's arm: "Tell him in Italian! Tell him we're lost and need help."

While the men spoke in Italian, I opened the door and got into the truck. I wanted to live the rest of my life there. Sitting on those lumpy springs was like experiencing a miracle. I wanted to marry the young Italian who owned the tinny truck and ride with him over the crest of the mountain and live with him in a farmhouse and never go back to the Palazzo Pucci with the insane stranger, my husband, who had snarled at me when I was exhausted and afraid. I didn't want to be alone with him in that freezing tomb, under the vicious, aristocratic faces of Pucci ancestors.

The truck driver got back in beside me, and my husband squeezed in from the passenger side. "He doesn't think there are any more houses ahead, but I told him we're only at 23 and we need number 99. He said to get in and we'd see what's up ahead." The truck started up and we drove forward into the black forest. Nothing lit the road but the headlights. The truck smelled of grease and the young man's body. *"Grazie, grazie,"* I said to him over and over. I could feel his hip against mine. My husband tried to take my hand, but I pulled away. We drove on, further and further from the Porta Romana, where that enormous woman stood in the middle of traffic wearing another huge woman on her head.

"Ecco," said the driver. We saw some lights, and then a wall, and then a door. The truck slowed and edged toward the wall. *"Novantanove!"* my husband cried jubilantly. "This is it!" He got out, pulling me after him. I wanted to give the young driver all our money, the pearly dolphin around my neck, the Gucci blouse off my back. My husband reached for his wallet. But the man smiled and dipped his

head at me. *"Signora,"* he said, *"grazie, no."* He shook my husband's hand warmly and drove off.

The famous harpsichordist answered the bell, this lunatic person who had not warned my husband that no one should ever try to take a bus to this place. The man was tall, stately, dignified, handsome. Fame and money had got him a home on a mountaintop. My husband was not famous or rich, and we lived in a plain house on a flat street. Luck, I felt, was unevenly distributed among human beings.

"We *walked* here from the Porta Romana," I said. "You didn't tell my husband we'd have to walk up a mountain."

"I did mention to him that it was best to take a cab."

"Well," I said. "He thought it best not to."

"Why don't you both come in?" he said, leading us through an open courtyard and into his villa, up a narrow staircase into a room with a high, domed ceiling, tile floors, and a harpsichord on each wall. I found a small bench and sat down at once. The famous man was telling my husband that the villa was built in the *Quattrocentro* and that he had had many difficulties in remodeling it. He mentioned grown children in the United States, and I wondered who lived here with him now, if anyone.

"Go ahead," he told my husband. "Try any of these instruments you like. This one is a Dowd, this square one is a Dutch-style virginal, a Skovroneck, and this is a genuine Stein fortepiano like the kind Mozart used, from about 1796." I didn't bother to look—I had seen enough harpsichords to last me all my life—but said to him, "Aren't you going to play them a little for us?" The man needed to understand the sacrifices we had made, the distance we had come, the dangers we had faced. In spite of my problems with my husband, I felt he should get what he had hoped for.

The harpsichordist shrugged, smiled condescendingly, turned his back, and disappeared down the stairs. His message seemed clear: *If you want to hear me perform, buy a ticket.*

My husband wandered around the room, sitting down to play some chords here and there, a few bars of the Bach English Suite he'd been practicing at home, a bit of Scarlatti. He seemed transfixed by each instrument, his ears cocked to its tones, his fingers stroking its ebony keys. He bent to examine the painted lids, the elaborate rose holes. He had forgotten I was in the room, forgotten how he had tortured me to get here and how I had almost died. I was expendable. He played the various instruments for about twenty minutes.

Unable to wait any longer, I went downstairs in search of a bathroom and met the famous man coming back up. He was carrying a small tray with food and wineglasses on it. "The bathroom?" I asked. He pointed downward and to the right. I found a tiny room with an ancient toilet, not clean, the seat up. He lived here alone.

The man served us squares of focaccia with green olives buried in the salty bread, along with some local red wine. He spoke briefly about his concert schedule, here and in the States. Then he stood up. Clearly, our visit was over; he had someplace to go. "It was nice to meet you—glad you could stop by." He gestured toward the door.

"I am not walking down that mountain," I announced.

The man stopped, puzzled. He thought for a moment. "Well, then, perhaps you should call a cab." He waited to see which of us would pull out a cell phone. Then he said, "I guess I'll have to call one for you."

He left the room and didn't return for ten minutes. When he did, he said with irritation, "There's no cab to be had at this hour. They don't want to drive up here when they have all the fares they need in the center."

"That's too bad," I said, staying seated.

"I'm sorry," my husband said, "to be so much trouble."

The man looked as if he agreed we'd been far too much trouble. "I suppose I'll have to take you down the mountain, then."

We followed him outside to his two-seater sports car. He pointed to another mountain across a valley. "The pianist Andres Schiff lives over there," he said.

"We don't plan to visit him," I said, for my husband's benefit.

The harpsichordist indicated that I would have to sit on my husband's lap for the trip down the mountain. He roared onto the road at an extremely high speed, taking hairpin turns like a racing-car driver. Curve after curve, I braced myself, falling to one side, then another. Was it possible we had walked up the mountain *this* far?

When we got to the bottom, to Porta Romana, he let us off. I felt he should have taken us ten minutes further, to San Marco, or even to our doorway on Via Ricasoli. Since we'd had no dinner, he could have been decent and bought us ice cream at the gelateria, the place where we had hid for safety the last time we had almost lost our lives. But the great man dropped us off at the bus stop, in view of the woman carrying her eternal burden, and sped away without so much as a wave.

We waited for the bus for a long, long time. The wind was very cold. My husband slumped against the wall and hung his head. He looked old and melancholy. After a while I leaned backward against his body. I felt as if I might faint. He turned me around and held my face in his hands. I let my body fall against his, my head on his shoulder. He promised that he would hail the first cab he saw.

We waited and waited, but none passed by. Then we saw the lights of the bus, and he stepped forward and held up his hand.

Minute Inventions

"This Is a Voice from Your Past"

Every woman gets a call like this sooner or later. The phone rings, a man says: "This is a voice from your past." If you're in the mood and the caller doesn't find you in a room where other people are (particularly your husband), and if you have some time to spare, you might enjoy playing the game.

"Who *is* this?" I said, when my call came.

"Don't you recognize my voice?"

"Not exactly."

"Alvord's class? Florida? Your senior year?"

I paused. There had been a number of young men in my life in college, in Florida, in my senior year—and most of them were in Alvord's class.

This call—the first from Ricky—came just after I had given birth to my second daughter; I was living in California. When the phone rang, I was in the kitchen cutting a hot dog into little greasy pieces for my two-year-old's lunch, and at the same time I felt my milk coming down, that sharp burning pain in both nipples, like an ooze of fire.

"Janet?" His voice was husky, or he was whispering. "This is a serious voice from your past. You know who I am. I think of you all the time. And I work at the phone company, I get free calls, so don't worry about this long-distance shit. I can talk to you all night if I want to."

"Tell me who you are," I said, just stalling for time, but suddenly I knew and was truly astounded. I had thought of Ricky often in the kind of reveries in which we all engage in when we count the lives that never were meant to be for us.

"You must know. I know you know."

" Well, it must be you, Ricky, isn't it? But *I* don't have all night. I have two babies now, and I'm feeding them right this minute."

"Is your old man there?"

"No."

"Good, get the kids settled down, and I'll hold on. And don't worry, I'm not going to complicate your life. I can't even get to you. I'm in Pennsylvania—and out of money."

"Hang on." I did some things I had to do for the children and then talked to him while my big girl ate in her high chair a foot away from the frayed green couch where I reclined on a pillow, letting the baby suck from my breast. Ricky told me then that he couldn't write a word anymore, it was killing him, he was drinking all the time, he had six kids, his wife was running around with someone else, and could I believe it, he, *he,* was working for the fucking phone company.

"I'm sorry," I said. "I'm really sorry, Ricky."

It occurred to me that anything else I might say, like "We all have to make compromises" or "Maybe at some point we have to give up our dreams," would sound trite. The fact was, I hadn't given up mine but had pursued it with a kind of dauntless energy. I didn't count the dream that he might have been my true love because I had known even then, all those years ago, that it was impossible. When he read his brilliant stories in class, he was married and living with his wife in a trailer on the outskirts of the campus. He'd already written his prize-winning story that had brought our writing-class to its knees, the one that was chosen later for an O. Henry Award.

Alvord, our professor, a famous and esteemed novelist himself, had informed us in class, in front of Ricky, that the boy had been touched by the wand of the muse—he spoke of Ricky as if a halo gleamed over his head. He made it clear that none of us would ever reach the heights (and should not hope to) for which this golden boy was destined. "A talent like his," he told us once, "is like a comet. It appears only once every hundred years or so."

I clung to my own modest talent, and I was working on it; I couldn't envy Ricky his, based as it was in Catholic guilt to which I had no access (his stories were all about sin and redemption); what I envied during that hungry, virginal senior year of college was his wife, the woman he held in his arms each night, the one whose face was caressed by the gaze of his deep-seeing, supernaturally wise marble-blue eyes.

The day he called me in California as I sat nursing my baby girl, feeling the electric suck of her pulsing lips sizzle in a lightning rod strike from nipple to womb, I remembered an image of Ricky that rose up like an illumination. We were in the university library. Ricky had come in alone and had chosen to sit across from me at one of the long mahogany tables where I was studying. He had his magic pencil in his long fingers and was bent over his lined notebook paper to create whatever piece of brilliant, remorse-filled prose he was writing. A long lock of his dirty-blond hair fell across his forehead, and his fingers scribbled, bent like crab pincers racing over the lined notebook page, wrote words that according to Alvord would turn out to be second only to James Joyce's.

Ricky had told me that his wife worked in some office, typing business documents. He explained, in his breathy East Coast accent, that she was ordinary and dull and that he had too young been seduced by her beauty, her astonishing breasts, and his own fierce desire. He assured me that I knew him in a way that she never could. We had long, earnest discussions after Alvord's class, and in the cafeteria over coffee, and on benches in front of the library—debates about literature and genius (who knows now if their content held anything more remarkable than youth and idealism cooked up in a predictable collegiate stew?).

Still, that night in the library, he stopped his work to stare intensely at me across the table time after time—but didn't smile. We were like conspirators, we knew we shared a plan, an ingenious plot to outfox time, mortality, death—we were both going to be famous writers, and we would—by our words alone—live forever.

At some point that evening, in his frenzy of writing, Ricky's cramped fingers relaxed, his head dropped sideways onto his arm on the table, and he fell asleep in the library. He remained there, vulnerable and naked in my gaze, breathing as I knew he must breathe as he slept beside his wife in that trailer, his mouth slightly open, his blue-veined eyelids closed over his blue eyes, his nostrils flaring slightly with each breath.

I watched him till the library closed, watched his face and memorized every line of his fair cheek, the angle of his chin, watched fascinated as a thin thread of drool spooled from his slightly parted lips to the tabletop. I looked around me to be sure no one was near or watching. Then, before he woke, I very slowly moved my hand across the table and anointed the tip of my pencil with his silver spit.

∝

The second time Ricky called me, my husband *was* in the room. It was thirty years later, a day in late August. I—with a slow but certain fortitude—had written and published a number of novels by then. My three daughters were grown. The baby who had been at my breast at the time of his first call was in graduate school, and older than I had been when Ricky slept opposite my gaze in the library.

"Janet? This is a voice from your past."

A warning bell rang in my chest. At that moment, I was busy talking to my husband about some family troubles (my mother had had a stroke and we were about to put her in a nursing home), and I felt rudely interrupted. I wasn't ready to engage in the game he wanted to play.

"Which past?" I said. "I have many."

"It's Ricky, your old buddy."

"Ricky! How are you?" I said his name with some enthusiasm because he expected it, but I felt my heart sink because I knew I would have to listen to his troubles, and I had no patience just then. The game of "remember what we meant to each other" had lost its appeal, since by this time everyone I loved filled up my life completely. I had not even a small chink of space left for a latecomer. "Are you still living in Pennsylvania?"

"No, I'm right here!"

"Right here?" I looked down into my lap as if I might find him there.

"In sunny California. In your very city. And I'm here for good."

"How did you know where to reach me? My number isn't even listed!"

"I found one of your books back east and on the cover it said what city you lived in. So when I got here—and I want you to know I picked this city to settle in because of *you*—I went to the library and asked the librarian. I knew a librarian was bound to know where the city's most famous writer lived. I told her I was your old buddy, and she gave me your phone number."

"I'm not famous, Ricky."

"Me neither," he said. "How about that?"

I told him I would call him back in half an hour—and in that time I explained to my husband, more or less, who he was. An old college friend. A used-to-be-writer. A drunk. I don't know why I dismissed Ricky so unfairly. Something in his voice had put me on guard. And I could see that this tag with time was a game there was no sense in playing. I had settled into my ordained life like concrete setting in a mold, and I no longer trifled with the idea that I might want to change it. At least not by trailing after romantic visions. With a sense of duty, though, I phoned him back . . . and braced myself.

"You won't believe the stuff that's happened to me," he said. He laughed—he almost cackled—and I shivered. "Can we get together?"

When I hesitated, he said, "I've been through AA; I'm a new person. I'm going to join up here, too, of course. The pity is that before I turned myself around I lost every friend I ever had."

"How come?"

"How come? Because an alcoholic will steal from his best friend if he has to; he'll lie with an innocent face like a newborn baby. There's nothing I haven't stooped to, Janet. I've been to the bottom; that's where you have to be before you can come back. I've rented a little room in town here, and I'm hoping . . . well, I'm hoping that we can be friends again."

"Well, why not," I said. I had the sense my house had become a tunnel, and I was getting lost in the dark.

"But mainly—I'm hoping you'll let me come to your class. I want to get started writing again."

"How did you know I teach a class?"

133

"It says on your book, Janet. That you teach writing at some university or other."

"Well, you certainly are a detective, aren't you?"

"I'm sly as a fox."

"I guess you could visit my class when it begins again after Labor Day. I'll tell my students that you studied with me in Alvord's class. Since most of my old students will be coming back to take the advanced class, they already know about Alvord. In fact, I quote him all the time. We use all his old terms—'action proper,' 'enveloping action'—his dedication to point of view. Maybe we can even get a copy of your old prize story and discuss it."

"Great. So when can we get this friendship on the road again?"

"Look—I'm having a Labor Day barbecue for my family and some friends on Sunday—why don't you come? Do you have a car?"

"I can borrow one."

"Do you need directions? I'll have my husband give them to you."

I called Danny to the phone and handed him the receiver. "Tell my friend Ricky the best way to get here." I wanted Ricky to hear Danny's voice, to know unequivocally that I was taken, connected, committed . . . that I wasn't under any circumstances available.

⌑

A stranger rang the doorbell, a man eighty years old, skin jaundiced, skeletal bones shaping his face. The golden hair was thin and gray. Only his voice, with an accent on his tongue like the young Frank Sinatra, convinced me he was the same Ricky. When I shook his hand, I felt his skin to be leathery, dry. When I looked down, the nails were bitten to the quick.

He came inside. I felt him take in the living room in one practiced glance—the artwork, the decorations, the furniture—and then we passed out the screen door to the backyard, where the party was in progress.

Danny was on the patio, grilling hamburgers and hot dogs over the coals. My three daughters, one already married and two home from their respective graduate schools, looked beautiful in their summer blouses and white shorts. I saw the backyard as Ricky must have seen it—alive with summer beauty, the plum tree heavy with purple fruit, the jasmine in bloom, the huge cactus plants in Mexican painted bowls growing new little shoots, fierce with baby spines.

My other guests included my sister and her sons, my eldest daughter's husband, a few of my students, several women I had been in a book club with for the past fifteen years. Ricky looked around; I could feel him adding up my life and registering it in his blood-shot eyes.

I took him over to meet Danny and then said: "Let's go sit on the swings and talk." We tramped across the brilliant green of the grass to the old swing set where my daughters used to play. Ricky was wearing a formal gray wool suit, his bony frame almost lost inside its wide shoulders. He swung slowly back and forth, sitting on the splintery wood seat, his hands clutching the rusty chains. He talked looking forward, into air.

"My son Bobby is the one who invited me out to California. He made it big-time," Ricky said and laughed.

"Is he in movies?" I asked.

"Not exactly. He dove into a city pool in Philly and broke his spine. Now he's in a wheelchair for life. I got him a sharp lawyer who brought a deep-pockets lawsuit against the city. Bobby was awarded a million and a half bucks, enough to take care of him the rest of his life and, if I play it right, take care of me, too! My other kids don't talk to me, so Bobby is my only salvation."

"But why is he in California?"

"He's living in a fantastic halfway house out here—the best in the world for paraplegics; Bobby gets all kinds of services, I even can bring my laundry over there and he'll get it done for me free. And he's got enough extra pocket money to help me pay my rent for a while 'til I get a job."

"What a terrible thing to happen to him."

"No, just the opposite. He was a beach bum, a loser. Now he's got it all together, the whole future taken care of. I think he's relieved. He can use his arms—he plays wheelchair basketball. He lifts weights. He gets counseling, he gets his meals served. Sometimes I wish I could change places with him. But, no, I'm back at square one, looking for a job again."

"No more phone company?"

Ricky made a strangling noise in his throat. "I'm going to write my novel, Janet. Finally. I'm going to get it together before I die. If I can sit in on your class, I figure it will start my motor again. You probably teach something like the way Alvord taught us. That old magic. Maybe I can feel that excitement again. I'm counting on it; it's my last hope."

"Do you ever hear from Alvord? Did you stay in touch?"

"In touch! I *lived* with him for a year in Florida when I was really down and out. He took me in, told me he loved me like a son. The trouble was he didn't feed me, Janet. He offered me a place to stay on this farm of his, and then all I could find to eat in the house was Campbell's soup. I think one day he actually hid the bacon from me so that I couldn't get my hands on it. So I had to take his truck into town with some money of his to get some food, but I'd been drinking again and I totaled it. He told me I had to leave. He gave me fifty bucks and bought me a train ticket back to Philly. But he was a pain, anyway, preaching to me all the time about being a man, taking responsibility for my kids. I swear, the man was a genius, but he's losing it, Janet. He's in his eighties now. He used to think I walked on water."

"We all did."

"That's why I came to live near you. You're the only one on earth who really knows my genius."

I didn't actually count, but I had the sense Ricky ate at least five hamburgers and as many hot dogs. He hung around the food table, his mouth going, not talking to anyone but looking at my women friends, their faces, their forms. He looked my daughters up and down—there was no way to stop him. At one point, he came to me and said, "Your daughters are really beautiful. All three of them. They have your soul in their eyes." I wanted to distract him. I asked him how often he saw his son; he said, "As often as I can, he gives me CARE packages. I don't have much food in the new place."

After our guests left, I packed up all the leftovers for Ricky: potato chips, lukewarm baked beans, the remaining coleslaw, a package of raw hot dogs and buns to go with them, a quarter of a watermelon, lettuce and sliced tomatoes, even pickles, even mustard and ketchup.

"Listen, thanks," he said. "You're a lifesaver. You don't know how lucky I feel to have found you again. Could I ask you one more favor, though? Would you mind if I came back tomorrow and used your typewriter? I need to write a letter to apply for a job. Someone gave me a tip about a job being night watchman in a truck yard. All I would have to do is sit in a little shed and watch for thieves. I figure I could write all night if I get it."

My reaction was instinctive; I knew I didn't want him back in my house again. "Why don't you let me lend you my electric typewriter? I use a computer now, so I won't need it for a while. I do love it, though—it's the typewriter I wrote my first novel on."

"Then maybe it will be lucky for me. I'll guard it with my life."

"Okay, give me a minute, I'll go put it in its case." I left him standing in the living room with my husband, but I heard no conversation at all—not even ordinary chatter. I could see why Danny was unable to think of a single thing to say to him.

Ricky finally left, laden like an immigrant—bags of food, paper, carbon paper, envelopes, stamps, my typewriter. He stuffed it all into the trunk of an old red car.

Danny and I watched him drive away. He didn't wave—he tore from the curb like one possessed.

"Funny guy," Danny said.

"I don't think we know the half of it," I told him.

⌘

I found Ricky's O. Henry prize story in a book and had thirty photocopies made for my students. At the start of class, I distributed the copies and told my students that at 7:30 a guest would be arriving, a writer of unique skill and vision, a man we were honored to have visit our class. I warned them about the pitfalls of the writer's life, how one could not count on it to earn a living, how so many talented writers fell by the wayside due to pressures of ordinary life. This visitor, I said, a very close friend of mine from the past who had missed what you might call "his window of opportunity," hoped to join our class and to work as hard as anyone in it. "He had a whole life in between of doing something else he had to do. All of you are young, at the start of your first lives, and if you really want this, this is the time to do it."

When Ricky arrived at my classroom, it was already almost 9:00 P.M. He apologized, saying the bus had been late. He was wearing a red V-necked sweater and looked less cadaverous than at the barbecue, but still much older than his years. He seemed elated to find that a copy of his story was on every desk, and when one of the students asked him how he had gotten the idea for it, he said, simply, "I had thought many times of murdering my brother."

By then, we were already in the midst of having another student read his story; I told the class that next week we would discuss Ricky's story.

I nodded for Harold to go on reading; his story was about a day in the cotton fields of Arkansas and how the men, women, and children picking cotton on a burning hot day react when the truck that delivers them fails to leave drinking water. When the last line had been read, Ricky spoke out in the exact tones of our teacher, Alvord.

"It comes alive on the last page, finally, you see, because it uses all the senses. Since a crying baby can seduce a reader from the very death of Hamlet himself, the writer must bring everything to life. And you do, young man! You do!"

The class was silent, and then a few students applauded Harold, and then everyone did — till his embarrassed smile lit up the room. I announced that we would take our usual ten-minute break. When the class had filed out, I thought I would find Ricky waiting to talk to me about my students, to tell me how the class had seemed to him, if it would suit his purposes. But he left the room without a glance in my direction, and, when I looked out into the hall, I saw him in deep conversation with one of my students, a young woman. When the class reconvened, neither one of them returned for the second half.

At seven the next morning, my student phoned me. "This is Alice Miller. I'm so sorry to disturb you," she said, "but your friend, the famous writer, borrowed my car last night. We went out for coffee, and afterward he said he had an urgent errand to go on; he practically got on his knees to beg to borrow the car. He said that although he knew I didn't know him very well, *you* could vouch for him, and he promised he would have my car back in my carport by midnight. He borrowed ten dollars, too. He never came back. And I can't get to work without it!"

"I'll see if I can reach him at the number I have for him," I told her. "I'm so sorry. I'll call you right back."

But his landlady did not find him in his room. I called Alice back and told her I could only imagine that there had been some emergency with his son, who was a paraplegic. I reassured her that he would surely have the car back to her very shortly but said in the meantime to take a taxi to work, that I would pay for it.

I learned later that, when finally Ricky did return the car to Alice, he never even rang her bell. He left the car at the curb. She found the inside of it littered with cigarette butts, racing forms, empty paper cups, and the greasy wrappers from McDonalds's hamburgers. The gas tank was totally empty. There was not even enough gas left in the tank for Alice to get to a gas station to fill it up.

⚮

Toward the end of September, I was about to apply for a fellowship and realized that I needed my typewriter to fill out the application form. My anger overcame my revulsion, and I dialed the number Ricky had originally given me. His landlady answered and informed me that he'd moved out bag and baggage—that "he shipped out to sea."

"To sea!" I imagined him on a whaling ship, thinking he was Melville or, more likely, that he was one of the sailors in Stephen Crane's story about men doomed at sea, "The Open Boat," a piece of work whose first line Alvord had often quoted: "None of them knew the color of the sky."

But my typewriter! I wanted it; it was mine. I felt as if Ricky had kidnapped one of my children.

"Let it go," my husband said. "It's an old typewriter, I'll get you a new one, it doesn't matter. Write it off as a business loss. Write him off—your old friend—if you can as one of those mistakes we all make in life."

In the days following, I had trouble sleeping. I held imaginary conversations with Ricky, by turns furious, accusatory, damning, murderous. "I trusted you!" I cried out, and in return I heard his laugh . . . his cackle. Alvord had often talked about evil in his class; the reality of it, how it existed, how it was as real as the spinning globe to which we clung.

Days later, in a frenzy, I began calling hospitals, halfway houses, rehab clinics, trying to find the place where Ricky's son lived—if indeed he had a son.

"Don't do this to yourself," Danny said. He saw me on the phone, sweating, asking questions, shaking with anger, trembling with outrage.

But one day I actually located the boy. He was in a hospital in a city only a half hour's drive from my house. I named his name, Bobby, with Ricky's last name, and someone asked me to wait, she would call him to the phone. And a man picked up the phone and said, "Yes? This is Bobby."

I told him I was a friend of his father, that his father had my typewriter.

"Oh sure, I know about that. You're his old friend. He left the typewriter here with me. You can come and get it." His voice had the same tones as Ricky's voice. The same seductive sound—the "Oh, sure" a kind of promise, the "come and get it," the serpent's invitation.

"His landlady said he went to sea?" I felt I must have another piece of the puzzle, at least one more piece.

"Yeah—he got a job teaching English on a navy ship. I told him he better take it; he wasn't going to freeload off me the rest of his life."

"I'm sorry," I said to the boy. "I'm sorry about your accident, and about your troubles with your father."

"Hey, don't worry about it. It's nothing new. But if you want his address on the ship, I could give it to you."

"No—thank you," I said. "I don't want it. I think your father and I have come to a parting of the ways. Good-bye, Bobby. I wish you good luck."

"You, too," Bobby said. "Anyone who knows my father needs it."

Then, two years after I talked to his son, I got the third phone call. "This is a voice out of your fucking past."

"Hello, Ricky." My heart was banging so hard I had to sit down.

"I heard from my son you want your goddamned typewriter back."

"No, no—"

"You'll have it back. It's in little pieces. I'll be on your doorstep with it in twenty minutes."

"I don't want it, Ricky. *Don't come here!* Keep it."

"I said you'll have it back. I *always* keep my word, you fucking . . ."

"Please, keep it. I don't need it! Keep it and write your book on it!"

"Just expect me," Ricky said. "I'll be there; you can count on it. Watch out your window for me."

And so I did. For a week. For a month. I keep watching and, sometimes, when the phone rings, I let it ring and don't answer it.

"I Don't Believe This"

After it was all over, one final detail emerged, so bizarre that my sister laughed crazily, holding both hands over her ears as she read the long article in the newspaper. I had brought it across the street to show it to her; now that she was my neighbor, I came to see her and the boys several times a day. The article said that the crematorium to which her husband's body had been entrusted for cremation had been burning six bodies at a time and dumping most of the bone and ash into plastic garbage bags that went directly into their dumpsters. A disgruntled employee had tattled.

"Can you imagine?" Carol said, laughing. "Even that! Oh, his poor mother! His poor *father*!" She began to cry. "I don't believe this," she said. That was what she had said on the day of the cremation, when she sat in my backyard in a beach chair at the far end of the garden, holding on to a washcloth. I think she was prepared to cry so hard that an ordinary handkerchief would not do. But she remained dry-eyed. When I came outside after a while, she said, "I think of his beautiful face burning, of his eyes burning." She looked up at the blank blue sky and said, "I just don't believe this. I try to think of what he was feeling when he gulped in that stinking gas. What could he have been thinking? I know he was blaming me."

She rattled the newspaper. A dumpster! Oh, Bard would have loved that. Even at the end, he couldn't get it right. Nothing ever went right for him, did it? And all along I've been thinking that I won't ever be able to swim in the ocean again because his ashes are floating in it! Can you believe it? How that woman at the mortuary promised they would play Pachelbel's *Canon* on the little boat, and the remains would be scattered with "dignity and taste"! His *mother* even came all the way down with that jar of his father's ashes that she had saved for thirty years so that father and son could be mixed together for all eternity. Plastic garbage bags! "You know," she said, looking at me, "life is just a joke, a bad joke, isn't it?"

❦

Bard had not believed me when I'd told him that my sister was in a shelter for battered women. Afraid of *him?* Running away from *him?* The world was full of dangers from which only *he* could protect her! He had accused me of hiding her in my house. "Would I be so foolish?" I had said. "She knows it's the first place you'd look."

"You better put me in touch with her," he had said menacingly. "You both know I can't handle this for long."

It had gone on for weeks. On the last day, he called me three times, demanding to be put in touch with her. "Do you understand me?" he threatened me. "If she doesn't call here in ten minutes, I'm checking out. Do you believe me?"

"I believe you," I said. "But you know she can't call you. She can't be reached in the shelter. They don't want the women there to be manipulated by their men. They want them to have space and time to think."

"Manipulated?" He was incredulous. "I'm checking *out,* this is *it*! Goodbye forever!"

He hung up. It wasn't true that Carol couldn't be reached. I had the number. Not only had I been calling her, but I had also been playing tapes for her of his conversations over the phone during the past weeks. This one I hadn't taped. The tape recorder was in a different room.

"Should I call her and tell her?" I asked my husband.

"Why bother?" he said. He and the children were eating dinner; he was becoming annoyed by this continual disruption in our lives. "He calls every day and says he's killing himself and he never does. Why should this call be any different?"

Then the phone rang. It was my sister. She had a fever and bronchitis. I could barely recognize her voice.

"Could you bring me some cough syrup with codeine tomorrow?" she asked.

"Is your cough very bad?"

"No, it's not too bad, but maybe the codeine will help me get to sleep. I can't sleep here at all. I just can't sleep."

"He just called."

"Really," she said. "What a surprise!" But the sarcasm didn't hide her fear. "What this time?"

"He's going to kill himself in ten minutes unless you call him."

"So what else is new?" She made a funny sound. I was frightened of her these days. I couldn't read her thoughts. I didn't know if the sound was a cough or a sob.

"Do you want to call him?" I was afraid to be responsible. "I know you're not supposed to."

"I don't know," she said. "I'm breaking all the rules anyway."

The rules were very strict. No contact with the batterer, no news of him, no worrying about him. Forget him. Only female relatives could call, and they were not to relay any news of him—not how sorry he was, not how desperate he was, not how he had promised to reform and never do it again, not how he was going to kill himself if she didn't come home. Once I had called the shelter for advice, saying that I thought he was serious this time, that he was going to do it. The counselor there, a deep-voiced woman named Katherine, said to me, very calmly, "It might just be the best thing; it might be a blessing in disguise."

My sister blew her nose. "I'll call him," she said. "I'll tell him I'm sick and to leave you alone and to leave me alone."

I hung up and sat down to try to eat my dinner. My children's faces were full of fear. I could not possibly reassure them about any of this. Then the phone rang again. It was my sister.

"Oh God," she said. "I called him. I told him to stop bothering you, and he said, *I have to ask you one thing, just one thing. I have to know this. Do you love me?*" My sister gasped for breath. "I shouted *No*—what else could I say? That's how I *felt*, I'm so sick, this is such a nightmare, and then he just hung up. A minute later I tried to call him back to tell him that I didn't mean it, that I did love him, that I *do*, but he was gone." She began to cry. "He was gone."

"There's nothing you can do," I said. My teeth were chattering as I spoke. "He's done this before. He'll call me tomorrow morning full of remorse for worrying you."

"I can hardly breathe," she said. "I have a high fever, and those boys are going mad cooped up here." She paused to blow her nose. "I don't believe any of this. I really don't."

⟨∞⟩

Afterward, she moved right across the street from me. At first she rented the little house, but then it was put up for sale, and my mother and aunt found enough money to make a down payment so that she could be near me and I could take care of her till she got her strength back. I could see her bedroom window from my bedroom window—we were that close. I often thought of her trying to sleep in that house, alone there with her sons and the new, big watchdog. She told me that the dog barked at every tiny sound and frightened her when there was nothing to be frightened of. She was sorry she had gotten him. I could hear his barking from my house, at strange hours, often in the middle of the night.

I remembered when she and I had shared a bedroom as children. We giggled every night in our beds and made our father furious. He would come in and threaten to smack us. How could he sleep, how could he go to work in the morning, if we were going to giggle all night? That made us laugh even harder. Each time he went back to his room, we would throw the quilts over our heads and laugh till we nearly suffocated. One night our father came to quiet us four times. I remember the angry hunch of his back as he walked, barefooted, back to his bedroom. When he returned the last time, stomping like a giant, he smacked us, each once, very hard, on our upper thighs. That made us quiet. We were stunned. When he was gone, Carol turned on the light and pulled down her pajama bottoms to show me the marks of his violence. I showed her mine. Each of us had our father's handprint, five red fingers, on the white skin of her thigh. She crept into my bed, where we clung to each other till the burning stinging shock subsided and we could sleep.

⟨∞⟩

Carol's sons, living on our quiet, adult street, complained to her that they missed the shelter. They rarely asked about their father and occasionally said they wished they could see their old friends and their old school. For a few weeks they had gone to a school hear the shelter; all the children had to go to school. But one day Bard had called me and told me he was trying to find the children. He said he wanted to take them out to lunch. He knew they had to be at some school. He was going to go to every school in the district and look in every classroom, ask everyone he saw whether any of the children there looked like his children. He would find them. "You can't keep them from me," he said, his voice breaking. "They belong to me. They love me."

Carol had taken them out of school at once. An art therapist at the shelter had held a workshop with the children every day. He was a gentle, soft-spoken man name Ned, who had the children draw domestic scenes and was never once surprised at the knives, bloody wounds, or broken windows that they drew. He gave each of them a special present, a necklace with a silver running-shoe charm, which only children at the shelter were entitled to wear. It made them special, he said. It made them part of a club to which no one else could belong.

While the children played with crayons, their mothers were indoctrinated by women who had survived, who taught the arts of survival. The essential rule was: "Forget him, he's on his own; the only person you have to worry about is yourself." A woman who was in the shelter at the same time as Carol had had her throat slashed. Her husband had cut her vocal cords. She could speak only in a grating whisper. Her husband had done it in the bathroom with her son watching. Yet, each night, she sneaked out and called her husband from a nearby shopping center. She was discovered and disciplined by the administration; they threatened to put her out of the shelter if she called him again. Each woman was allowed space at the shelter for a month while she got legal help and made new living arrangements. Hard cases were allowed to stay a little longer. She said she was sorry, but he was the sweetest man, and when he loved her up, it was the only time she knew heaven.

Carol felt humiliated. Once each week, the women lined up and were given their food: three very small whole frozen chickens, a package of pork hot dogs, some plain-wrap cans of baked beans, eggs, milk, margarine, white bread. The children were happy with the food. Carol's sons played in the courtyard with the other children. Carol had difficulty relating to the other mothers. One had ten children. Two had black eyes. Several were pregnant. She began to have doubts that what Bard had done had been violent enough to cause her to run away. Did mental violence or violence done to furniture really count as battering? She wondered if she had been too hard on her husband. She wondered if she had been wrong to come here. All he had done—he said so himself, on the taped conversations, dozens of times—was to break a lousy hundred-dollar table. He had broken it before; he had fixed it before. Why was this time different from any of the others? She had pushed all his buttons, that's all, and he had gotten mad, and he had pulled the table away from the wall and smashed off its legs and thrown the whole thing outside into the yard. Then he had put his head through the wall, using the top of his head as a battering ram. He had knocked open a hole to the other side. Then he had bitten his youngest son on the scalp. What was so terrible about that? It was just a momentary thing. He didn't mean anything by it. When his son had begun to cry in fear and pain, hadn't he picked up the child and told him it was nothing? If she would just come home, he would never get angry again. They'd have their sweet life. They'd go to a picnic, a movie, the beach. They'd have it better than ever before. He had just started going to a new church that was helping him to become a kinder and more sensitive man. He was a better person than he had ever been; he now knew the true meaning of love. Wouldn't she come back?

༺⚮༻

One day Bard called me and said, "Hey, the cops are here. You didn't send them, did you?"

"*Me?*" I said. I turned on the tape recorder. "What did you do?"

"Nothing. I busted up some public property. Can you come down and bail me out?"

"How can I?" I said. "My children. . . ."

"How can you *not*?"

I hung up and called Carol at the shelter. I told her, "I think he's being arrested."

"Pick me up," she said, "and take me to the house. I have to get some things. I'm sure they'll let me out of the shelter if they know he's in jail. I'll check to make sure he's really there. I have to get us some clean clothes and some toys for the boys. I want to get my picture albums. He threatened to burn them."

"You want to go to the house?"

"Why not? At least we know he's not going to be there. At least we can know we won't find him hanging from a beam in the living room."

We stopped at a drugstore a few blocks away and called the house. No one was there. We called the jail. They said their records showed that he had been booked, but they didn't know for sure whether he'd been bailed out. "Is there any way he can bail out this fast?" Carol asked.

"Only if he uses his own credit card," the man answered.

"I *have* his credit card," Carol said to me after she hung up. "We're so much in debt that I had to take it away from him. Let's just hurry. I hate this! I hate sneaking into my own house this way."

I drove to the house, and we held hands going up the walk." I feel his presence is here, that he's right here seeing me do this," she said, in the dusty, eerie silence of the living room. "Why do I give him so much power?" It's as if he knows whatever I'm thinking, whatever I'm doing. When he was trying to find the children, I thought he had eyes like God and that he would go directly to the school where they were and kidnap them. I had to warn them, 'If you see your father anywhere, run and hide. Don't let him get near you!' Can you imagine telling your children that about their father? Oh, God, let's hurry."

She ran from room to room, pulling open drawers, stuffing clothes into paper bags. I stood in the doorway of their bedroom, my heart pounding as I looked at their bed with its tossed covers, at the phone he used to call me. Books were everywhere on the bed— books about how to love better, how to live better, books on the occult, on meditation, books on self-hypnosis for peace of mind. Carol picked up and open book and looked at some words underlined in red. "You can always create your own experience of life in a beautiful and enjoyable way if you keep your love turned on within you—regardless of what other people say or do," she read aloud. She tossed it down in disgust. "He's paying good money for these," she said. She kept blowing her nose.

"Are you crying?"

"No!" she said. "I'm allergic to all this dust."

I walked to the front door, checked the street for his car, and went into the kitchen.

"Look at this," I called to her. On the counter was a row of packages, gift-wrapped. A card was slipped under one of them. Carol opened it and read it aloud: "I have been a brute and I don't deserve you. But I can't live without you and the boys. Don't take that away from me. Try to forgive me." She picked up one of the boxes and then set it down. "I don't believe this," she said. "God, where are the children's picture albums! I can't *find* them." She went running down the hall. In the bathroom, I saw the boys' fish bowl, with their two goldfish swimming in it. The water was clear. Beside the bowl was a piece of notebook paper. Written on it in his hand were the words "Don't give up, hang on, you have the spirit within you to prevail."

⁂

Two days later, he came to my house, bailed out of jail with money his mother had wired. He banged on my front door. He had discovered that Carol had been to the house. "Did *you* take her there?" he demanded. "*You* wouldn't do that to me, would you?" He stood on the doorstep, gaunt, his hands shaking.

"Was she at the house?" I asked. "I haven't been in touch with her lately."

"Please," he said, his words slurred, his hands out for help. "Look at this." He showed me his arms; the veins in his forearms were black and blue. "When I saw Carol had been home, I took the money my mother sent me for food and bought three packets of heroin. I wanted to OD. But it was lousy stuff, it didn't kill me. It's not so easy to die, even if you want to. I'm a tough bird. But, please,

149

can't you treat me like regular old me; can't you ask me to come in and have dinner with you? I'm not a monster. Can't anyone, *anyone,* be nice to me?"

My children were hiding at the far end of the hall, listening. "Wait here," I said. I went and got him a whole cooked chicken I had. I handed it to him where he stood on the doorstep and stepped back with distaste. Ask him in? Let my children see *this*? Who knew what a crazy man would do? He must have suspected that I knew Carol's exact whereabouts. Whenever I went to visit her at the shelter, I took a circuitous route, always watching in my rearview mirror for his blue car. Now I had my tear gas in my pocket; I carried it with me all the time, kept it beside my bed when I slept. I thought of the things in my kitchen: knives, electric cords, mixers, graters, stove elements that could become white-hot and sear off a person's flesh.

He stood there like a supplicant, palms up, eyebrows raised in hope, waiting for a sign of humanity from me. I gave him what I could—a chicken and a weak, pathetic little smile. I said, dishonestly, "Go home. Maybe I can reach her today; maybe she will call you once you get home." He ran to his car, jumped in it, sped off, and I thought, coldly, "Good, I'm rid of him. For now we're safe." I locked the door with three locks.

Later, Carol found among his many notes to her one that said, "At least your sister smiled at me, the only human thing that happened in this terrible time. I always knew she loved me and was my friend."

He became more persistent. He staked out my house, not believing I wasn't hiding her. "How could I possibly hide her?" I said to him on the phone. "You know I wouldn't lie to you."

"I know you wouldn't," he said. "I trust you." But on certain days I saw his blue car parked behind a hedge a block away, saw him hunched down like a private eye, watching my front door. One day my husband drove away with one of our daughters beside him, and an instant later the blue car tore by. I got a look at him then, curved over the wheel, a madman, everything at stake, nothing to lose, and I felt he would kill, kidnap, hold my husband and children hostages till he got my sister back. I cried out. As long as he lived, he would search for her, and, if she hid, he would plague me. He had once said to her (she told me this), "You love your family? You want them alive? Then you'd better do as I say."

✑

On the day he broke the table, after his son's face crumpled in terror, Carol told him to leave. He ran from the house. Ten minutes later, he called my sister and said, in the voice of a wild creature, "I'm watching some men building a house, Carol. I'm never going to build a house for you now. Do you know that?" He was panting like an animal. "And I'm coming back for you. You're going to be with me one way or another. You know I can't go on without you."

She hung up and called me. "I think he's coming back to hurt us."

"Then get out of there," I cried, miles away and helpless. "Run!"

By the time she called me again, I had the number of the shelter for her. She was at a gas station with her children. Outside were two phone booths—she hid her children in one; she called the shelter from the other. I called the boys at the number in their booth, and I read to them from a book called *Silly Riddles* while she made arrangements to be taken in. She talked for almost an hour to a counselor at the shelter. All the time I was sweating and reading riddles. When it was settled, she came into the children's phone booth and we made a date to meet in forty-five minutes at Sears so that she could buy herself some underwear and her children some blue jeans. They were still in their pajamas.

Under the bright fluorescent lights in the department store, we looked at price tags, considered quality and style, while her teeth chattered. Our eyes met over the racks, and she asked me, "What do you think he's planning now?"

✑

My husband got a restraining order to keep him from our doorstep, to keep him from dialing our number. Yet he dialed it, and I answered the phone, almost passionately, each time I heard it ringing, having run to the phone where I had the tape recorder hooked up. "Why is she so afraid of me? Let her come to see me without bodyguards! What can happen? The worst I could do is to kill her, and how bad could that be, compared with what we're going through now?"

I played her that tape. "You must never go back," I said. She agreed; she had to. I brought clean nightgowns to her at the shelter; I brought her fresh vegetables, and bread that had substance.

Bard hired a psychic that last week and went to Las Vegas to confer with him, bringing a $500 money order. When he got home, he sent a parcel to Las Vegas, containing clothing of Carol's and a small gold ring that she often wore. A circular that Carol found later under the bed promised immediate results: "Gold has the strongest psychic power — you can work a love spell by burning a red candle and reciting 'In this ring I place my spell of love to make you return to me.' This will also prevent your loved one from being unfaithful."

⌒◈⌒

Carol moved across the street from my house just before Halloween. We devised a signal so that she could call me for help in case some maniac cut her phone lines. She would use the antique gas alarm that our father had given to me. It was a loud wooden clacker that had been used in the war. She would open her window and spin it. I could hear it easily. I promised her that I would look out of my window often and watch for suspicious shadows near the bushes under her windows. Somehow, neither of us believed he was really gone. Even though she had picked up his wallet at the morgue, the wallet he'd had with him while he breathed his car's exhaust through a vacuum cleaner hose, thought his thoughts, told himself she didn't love him and so he had to do this and do it now, even though his ashes were in the dumpster, we felt that he was still out there, still looking for her.

Her sons built a six-foot-high spider web out of heavy white yarn for a decoration and nailed it to the tree in her front yard. They built a graveyard around the tree, with wooden crosses. At their front door, they rigged a noose and hung a dummy from it. The dummy, in their father's old blue sweatshirt with a hood, swung from the rope. It was still there long after Halloween, still swaying in the wind.

Carol said to me, "I don't like it, but I don't want to say anything to them. I don't think they're thinking about him. I think they just made it for Halloween, and they still like to look at it."

"Tell Me Your Secret"

The time was the fifties, and everything we young women did was fraught with danger. We could get pregnant, we could get raped, we could get lost, we could get seduced, our boyfriends could beg us to iron all their shirts for a year and then not marry us after all. We couldn't get diaphragms without a doctor's appointment but couldn't ask to be fitted for one unless we were about to be married. If we somehow—heaven forbid—became pregnant, we'd heard that Puerto Rico was the only place we could get an abortion that wouldn't kill us. We were suspected of lascivious behavior as a matter of fact: the campus dress code was rigid and demanded that we not wear shorts more than one inch above the knee, and then only under a nontransparent raincoat and only for essential sporting events. The dorm mothers rushed around the lounges where we met our young men, ordering us to keep "all four feet on the floor at all times." And, of course, no men, not even our fathers, were allowed into our dorm rooms.

Those of us who aspired to education learned soon enough that the college administrators at our Florida university were seriously unwilling to give graduate fellowships or teaching assistantships to women, convinced as they were that we'd run off and get married and that men were better risks and more deserving in every case.

Our mothers let us know that they hoped for the best, especially that we would be engaged before graduation, since afterward, because we'd all be elementary school teachers, the chances of our meeting marriageable men would be negligible. Our fathers, knowing how men are, feared the worst, that we would lose our virginity before being spoken for, but none of them—being men themselves—ever talked to us face-to-face about their concerns.

In spite of all this, I kept humming along in a little cocoon of self-direction, certain that none of society's prescriptions for me were going to affect my future. I would get a fellowship if I wanted one, a husband and babies in the right order if I wanted them, and no one I didn't want to get my virginity would get it. I would stay as innocent as I wanted to be for as long as I wanted to be.

An event that upset my grip on this blind certainty happened on a Saturday in the month of May, just before final exams of my junior year. I was in my dorm room ironing a dotted-Swiss pink party dress with fitted bodice and scoop neck and a little white bow at its center. I had just come back from town, where I'd bought pink leather flats to go with my dress, and I'd also had my hair cut short so that—with just a toss of my fingers—curls would shimmer all over my head. I was twenty years old and as pretty as I would ever be in this life.

Tonight, in the woods at the edge of town, there would be a party at the home of my psychology professor, Barton Flack, a bearded and attractive man, who, in the classroom, sat on the edge of his desk, tapping his shined loafers against the wooden desk edge as he lectured. He was famous for inventing a board game that was selling out all over the country and making him a millionaire. With the proceeds, Barton (as he asked us to address him in the interests of equality) had built a modern glass and wood house deep in a forest of Florida pines, with bedrooms separate from the house and ringing the living area like a circle of motel rooms. (He raised his brows suggestively when he described these rooms to the girls who hung around his desk after class.)

He had intimated all semester that when school was out, he'd throw a party like none other, and a couple of his selected favorites would be invited to meet some mystery guests, friends of his from the intellectual and art worlds who would surely raise a few hairs on our heads.

Iconoclast that he was, he still had to get around authoritarian rule: girls had to be back in the dorms by curfew. He had to figure out how we could spend the night at his place. We told him we lived under a microscope: each time we left for the evening, we were required to sign out on a card kept in a box at the reception desk. We had to state our destination, the name of our companion(s), and our expected time of return. When we came back (if we had the good fortune not to get seduced and left for dead in the lime quarry), we had to certify and initial our time of return.

Barton arranged a deception for me and another student of his by inveigling a couple of his women friends to pretend they were our "aunts" who would appear before the dorm mothers and testify in writing that they were our relatives and were taking us off campus for a night of wholesome and purely educational activities. The opera, perhaps. The other girl, Diane Weinberger, who also lived in my dorm, had agreed to cooperate in the plot. She was not my friend, this short, plain, ordinary-looking girl who never wore make-up, who wore glasses, who was a math major, and who had the distinct look of a lesbian about her (or so some said; I had no experience with lesbians, so left it to those who knew better). Barton seemed to admire her serious demeanor, her powerful mind, and her indifferent dress—she seemed an iconoclast also—at a time when there weren't many around who were girls.

∞

As I prepared for the party, ironing my dress and packing a small overnight case with clothes for the next day, my roommate, Flora Lu Matterfield, sat like a hippopotamus on her bed wearing her elastic chin-lift device and watched me with a look of despair on her face.

"Honeybun, I'm worried about you, going to that man's house for the night, with God knows what's going to happen out there in the woods. You know that man has a reputation! He knows female psychology, he's famous for it, so that's why he can convince you you're going out there for some so-called party when he could be planning to sell you down the river into white slavery. Otherwise, why wouldn't he want to get you back here safe and sound by curfew?" Her mouth, held in an unnatural position by the elastic straps, caused her to speak as if she were under water.

"Parties in the real world don't even get *started* till around midnight, Flora Lu. How can I expect him—*the host*—to deliver me back here by curfew?"

"Well, if they find your body in the swamp," Flora Lu said lugubriously, "I refuse to testify in court and say I warned you. I won't muddy your name. I'll just pretend I never saw you pack your little pink lacy nightgown in that little case. I didn't see a thing."

"It's not lace. It's cotton flannel, Flora Lu."

"In the dark, who will know the difference?"

Flora Lu was frowning and mumbling to herself and leafing through *Bride* magazine and I was putting the finishing touches on my dress when the room buzzer sounded. I went to the intercom and buzzed back.

"Special delivery for Franny at the front desk."

"I'll be right down." I tried to imagine who would send me a special delivery package. Maybe I was being notified that I'd won a poetry contest I'd entered. Maybe it was from Ted, a young man with whom I'd been pen pals for years. He liked to shock me by sending bizarre packages. Once, after he visited Italy, he sent me little sealed bottles of polluted water from the Venetian canals.

The girl at the desk handed me a blue airmail envelope, with scrawls all over it that said: "Rush! Private! Urgent! Personal!" The return address was that of Billy Carp, a childhood friend of mine who still lived in Brooklyn, where I'd grown up. I took the letter upstairs and read the first sentence: "Dear Franny, I saw your grandmother this morning and I will see her again this afternoon." This puzzled me. Why would Billy see her in any case? She was eighty-seven years old; I hadn't seen her in several years, myself. She was in a nursing home, paralyzed by a stroke. My aunt lived nearby and visited her daily. My aunt and Billy's mother were friends, but Billy was at Brooklyn College and wouldn't normally be seeing my grandmother.

"No one here wanted to tell you this, but I feel it's my duty as your friend to be sure you know the truth. Your parents have always protected you from the realities of life, whereas my mother always let me have it right up front, from the day my father died when I was twelve to the lovers my mother brought home when I was in high school."

Feeling alarmed, I turned the page over and read the end of the letter.

"She was old, anyway, and her life wasn't worth much. Don't lose too much sleep over this. It's the way of the world. Love from your good friend, Billy." Now I scanned the letter in panic, looking for the operational phrase, which finally I found. "Your grandmother died today of massive blood loss from bleeding ulcers. Your folks didn't plan to tell you this till after you finished your final exams. I went with my mother and your aunt to the hospital this morning, and we'll be going to the Jewish Funeral Home this afternoon."

I sat down on my bed.

"Honey, you're white as a ghost. Tell Flora Lu what's wrong."

"My grandmother died."

"Lord a mercy," she said. She put down her magazine. "Well, I guess you can just forget your little party now." She stared at my face and then pulled off her chin-lift device. "Honey, you stay here with me, and I'll take good care of you. We'll light a little candle and pray together for her precious soul that just passed on."

I left my room, walked out the back door of the dorm, and followed the path out to the miniature golf course. I looked up: trees, sky. The great glory of Nature. Death. Death was part of Nature. I knew I wasn't feeling the proper emotions. This was bad news. My mother's mother dead. Someday it would be my mother, then me. I kept pushing myself into different slots, trying to know what to feel. Where were my tears? Where was my heart? Why wasn't I crying? Why, in fact, was I was thinking about my pink dress and worrying that now I probably wouldn't get to wear it tonight? I suddenly remembered my father's older sister, my aunt who had committed a terrible crime in our family. I'd heard her black heart cursed many times: "Did you know that the night her mother died your Aunt Ruth actually went to a party?" It was the worst that could be said about her—this horror she had committed, this taint she had brought down on the family. Privately, I had always thought it wasn't such a bad thing to do: if you had a party to go to and someone died, why not go to your party? The dead wouldn't particularly care, would they? If they loved you, they'd want you to go on having your life.

I definitely wanted to have my life. In fact, I had a feeling that some part of it was actually going to start tonight, at the party. My anger swung toward Billy. Why hadn't he minded his own business? Now I had an obligation to feel bad. I'd have to call home and argue with my parents, blaming them for treating me like a child. I would get upset, I might cry, I'd lose my dreamy party rhythm (I was losing it already), and I'd be too far gone to think of going anywhere.

Maybe I could just pretend the letter hadn't arrived. It was just a matter of information. Why not imagine I simply didn't know about this death and continue to feel happy? I could go back upstairs and choose which necklace to wear to decorate the scoop neckline of the dress—a small, final act of grace I had been looking forward to all day. If only I hadn't told Flora Lu!

I looked up at the dorm windows, and I felt that, against my will, the entire landscape of my world had changed. I was now obligated to think about the meaning of death, the short span of life, how life was, as we had learned in Shakespeare class, "a walking shadow, a poor player that struts and frets his hour upon the stage and then is heard no more . . . a tale told by an idiot, full of sound and fury, signifying nothing . . ."

Right now I was supposed to be shedding tears, trying to remember little things about my grandmother and starting to miss her. I also should probably be thinking about God and his role in all this, if there was a God and if he had a role. This was all very far from my present interests. Light years away. The deeper meanings of life seemed totally irrelevant to me. Why should I waste my time on such useless pondering?

⸙

At 8:00 P.M., as soon as the buzzer rang in my room, I hurried out with my little suitcase, despite Flora Lu's pronouncement that I was bound to go to hell for this. The "aunt" who came to sign me out at the front desk wore an emerald-green satin dress, gold earrings shaped like serpents, and sling-back suede high heels. As I came down the ramp into the lobby, she teetered toward me in little mincing steps because of the narrowness of her dress and held her arms out to embrace me. As she hugged me to her visibly pointed breasts, waves of her perfume blazed into my eyes and made them tear. Since she apparently had already completed her paperwork with the dorm mother, she put her arm around me, took my overnight case in her free hand, and walked me toward the door. Just then, Diane Weinberger arrived in the lobby, and I saw a woman in a navy blue suit and carrying an alligator handbag rise from a chair and walk toward her. Another embrace took place: Diane stood like a stick of concrete while the woman exclaimed about how pretty she looked. (Diane was dressed in brown corduroy pants and a man's plaid shirt.)

"Shall we go?" my new friend advised. She led me out the door. I gave myself up to her, let her put me into her red sports car, let her speed away into the night with me, and allowed her to deliver me into the labyrinth of the professor's dark woods.

◈

All of the guests at the party, standing in the circular, brightly lit living room, holding drinks and paper plates of food, were reflected back upon themselves by the great panes of glass that looked out into the black forest. It seemed a scene from a horror movie: while they were all blindly chattering away and eating hors d'oeuvres, the woods were closing in on them like an iron trap and would shortly devour them.

I would surely be afraid to live here myself, walking alone through the house at night, reading unprotected in the glare of the bright lights, while outside, surrounding me, the mysterious woods hid whatever eyes might be looking in at me.

Barton had furnished his new house with orange furniture—strangely shaped plastic orange tables, orange canvas cloth laid over black metal chair frames, orange Chinese paper lanterns, orange ash trays. My professor circulated among his guests; he was smoking a cigar. His shoes were especially highly polished, his beard neatly trimmed and pointed, giving him a little air of the devil. He put his arm around me and told me I looked beautiful.

Leading me around the circular room, he introduced me to his friends: a South American diplomat (a tall, hairy, bearlike man with a sweet smile), an actress (the woman in green satin who was my "aunt"), a poet, a playwright, the owner of an alligator farm, a professor of philosophy.

Diane Weinberger stood under an orange paper lantern talking to the diplomat; her hands hung at her sides, holding neither cup nor plate. The man kept offering his plate to her, and finally he picked up a shrimp wrapped in bacon and popped it into her mouth. When she had swallowed, she opened her mouth for another.

Music was playing: Yma Sumac singing one of her weird and unearthly songs—she was a woman whose voice had an uncanny range, from bass to highest soprano. I'd heard her on the radio; she gave me the feeling that if I listened to her too long, I would be driven insane.

I told myself that I was finally at the professor's party, the party I had so badly wanted to attend and for which I had prepared for days, the party that promised so much and for which I had betrayed the moral teachings of my upbringing and made an enemy of my roommate. Since I was here, I was duty-bound to enjoy myself. And if Diane Weinberger—a girl as Jewish as I was—could eat shrimp and bacon, so could I. I piled my plate high. I ate at least a dozen of these delicacies; they were delicious, the white, chewy, forbidden shrimp circled by the fried, crisp, salty flesh of pig.

⌒∞⌒

There was dancing and drinking long into the night. No one danced with me, but I sat in an orange chair and watched those who did dance. Barton and the actress-in-satin moved their bodies together in ways I didn't know was possible. At some point, during a lull in the music, my professor brought out his board game, and we all sat down on the orange rug in a circle to play his invention, "Tell Me Your Secret."

There was the traditional game board and the conventional die to throw. Unlike Monopoly, which frequently sent you to jail, this game had instructions on the board to "go back to your mother's womb" or "confess in the palace of dreams" or "take a card from the treasure cave."

The cards were dangerous as quicksand: they required that each player tell a secret. "Tell your most embarrassing memory." "Tell about the time you stole something from a store." "Tell about the night you saw your parents in bed together." "Tell about the first time you played doctor as a child." Each time a member of the party hesitated, Barton would pour his guest another glass of champagne, and the others would urge him on. There was much laughter and then, eventually, a secret was blurted out, after which there was even more laughter. The things I heard were shocking to me; I felt I needed a long time to think about each confession, to understand what its impact on the person might have been. Everyone else, though, would listen to a confession, laugh knowingly, and then look up, ready and waiting for the next revelation.

My turn was coming up soon. The South American diplomat told of how, when he was fourteen, he had had sex with his cousin, a woman of twenty-five. Diane Weinberger revealed that her older brother used to read dirty stories to her and then gave her a nickel to rub his penis "till it popped and the scum came out." She stated this with cool satisfaction. Then she admitted she didn't think any man could ever excite her as much as her brother had in their youth.

How could I play this game? What comparable thing could I say—that I had once read a scene in a novel called "God's Little Acre" about a girl getting spanked with a hairbrush and it interested me unduly so that I read it over several times and still remembered it? Or that I had taken a quarter from the dresser of one of my girlfriends and hid it in my sock when I was eleven years old? I began to think of Flora Lu with longing; oh to be back in my dorm room, safe under the blankets, the lights long out after the more-than-reasonable curfew, which was designed for my own good!

Now some truth would be extracted from me and transform me in the minds of others—and even in my own—into a different person. In the next few moments, I would lose my privacy forever.

The die were put in my hands by my professor. "Have courage!" he whispered to me. "The truth will set you free."

I cast the die. I moved my game piece. I chose my card and read it.

"Tell the thing you are most ashamed of."

I looked around the circle at the faces of the guests who now seemed to wait in judgment for my confession. All the players had their eyes upon me; their mouths seemed loose and limp, hanging open with lascivious hunger.

"I came to this party," I said, "even though I just learned today . . . I came here even though . . . my grandmother died." I waited for the glass walls of the professor's house to implode, for one of the glass shards to pierce my heart. I thought of my mother, brokenhearted at home, and of my father, who would have died of grief to see me here, besotted with champagne and fattened to bursting with bacon and shrimp.

"How old was she?" the actress asked.

"She was eighty-seven."

"Oh, well. That doesn't count, then; you can't be guilty about *that*!" she said. "She lived long enough. It has to be something you're really ashamed of."

"It counts." Barton defended me. He came and knelt beside me and put his arm around my shoulder. "She *is* ashamed. That's what Franny has to tell you. That's what you have to accept. The rules of the game are that you can't challenge what someone feels is her truth."

I passed the die to the next person in the circle. She tossed them, and I was forgotten. I excused myself and went to find the orange bathroom where all the little orange soaps were in the shapes of women's breasts. I wanted to cry, but I had had too much champagne to be able to get near the place where my tears resided.

⌘

It was nearly dawn, and I was half-asleep in a chair when the actress offered to lead me to my guest room for the night. Just as we had heard, the bedrooms were separate from the house, arranged in a row of motel-like rooms, their walls, like those in the house, made entirely of glass that looked out into the woods on two sides. I went into the bathroom, which adjoined the guest room on the other side, and locked both doors in order to get undressed out of view of the windows, to put on my cotton flannel nightgown and to brush my teeth like a good girl. Through the door, I could hear the voices of Diane Weinberger and the South American diplomat. He had a deep booming laugh, like rolling thunder. Her laugh was high and whiny but full of a strange, giddy joy. Soon they stopped talking and began gasping and guffawing breathlessly as if they were tickling one another.

I got into bed and shut off the bedside lamp as fast as possible. With the light off, I could see a few feet into the woods by the glow of light coming from the next room. The pine trees were enormous, weighted down by Spanish moss that waved in the wind like witches' hair.

From the other side of the wall, I could hear the noises of Diane Weinberger and the hairy man. I could hear the bedsprings rumble, I could hear her high cries and his low groans. I listened, totally alert, for a very long time. Holding onto the sides of my bed, I traveled with them on their ride, their slow, deliberate journey over the twists and turns of the tracks, inching up the roller coaster to the screaming, blinding pitch of sensation. After their last screams, someone turned off the light in their room, plunging the woods into darkness.

I lay there, hot in my bed under the sheet, smelling the scent of sawdust from the new wood flooring. Heat lightning flashed in the sky, and the rumble of thunder vibrated through the room. With every flash of light, I thought I saw a face looking in the huge window. I begged myself to go to sleep.

Through the glass, I watched the full moon riding under and over the blowing storm clouds till it was buried in blackness. Again I saw a face at my window. The door, which had no lock on it, opened slowly, and Barton Flack's voice whispered my name.

"Franny? Are you awake? There's a big storm blowing in. It can get pretty fierce out here; I didn't want you to be afraid."

"I'm not afraid," I said.

My professor came and sat down on the edge of my bed. He was wearing some kind of loose caftan; he found my hand and began to stroke my arm.

"This has been a very strange night for you, Franny," he said. "I know you've been very, very careful in your life so far. I just want to tell you—there's no prize for being careful." He reached up and touched my face. Then he leaned forward, cupped my head in his hands, and kissed my lips very gently. "You could come into bed with me and my friend," he said. "We could ride out the storm together. It could be one of our secrets."

He waited for my answer. After a great burst of lightning, the moon appeared again in the sky. My white-haired grandmother was by now deep under the ground, cold as stone, still as stone, giving up her soft flesh to the history of the earth. "The sun shall not smite her by day, nor the moon by night," I heard in my mind. My own history was just beginning. How short a time lay ahead to be under sun and moon.

My professor was standing now beside my bed, his hand extended to me. "Come," he invited me. "We will enjoy the night."

After a moment, I let him pull me to my feet.

An Unfinished Autobiography

A Few Words

They had lost so many by the time I was born. My mother had lost her father and her brother. My grandmother had lost her first husband, her second husband, and her son. My aunt, who lived with us, had (also) lost her father and her brother. By the time I was five, my mother had, in addition, lost her nephew and her stillborn son; my aunt (if you count the dead baby) had lost two nephews and my grandmother, likewise, two grandsons. Each counted her own losses fully; the overlap seemed merely to increase the number of snatched-away souls. Their combined ghostly mass in our home was cumulative and oppressive. The women who raised me hovered about me in fear and mourning. The awareness of loss sustained and loss yet to come was my first impression of the nature of life.

My household was volatile: my mother explosive, my father conciliatory (he had to be), my aunt and grandmother (who lived upstairs while I lived with my parents downstairs) acting as buffers or mediators or simply as "flies on the wall." There was no telling what a day would bring. I spent my childhood in a heightened state of awareness, the better to predict when to take cover or to guess from what quarter the explosion would come. At times I would try to hide from it; at others I would decide how to cause it. I took it all in. I made my judgments, assessments, drew my conclusions. I didn't let down my guard very often—they all depended on me to keep things going. I ran from the downstairs to the upstairs to the downstairs, checking the positions and states of mind of the major players, keeping the house in balance.

Merrill Joan Gerber, age three, with her father, William Gerber, Brooklyn, 1941.

I knew I was pivotal, an important property. My aunt, single, childless, wanted me and wanted my father, too. My mother, who had me, was gifted with little patience. They all coveted me, fought over me, bargained for me, courted me. My sister wasn't born till I was seven, so I had their undiluted attention for years. And they had mine.

My fiction does, of course, take a good deal of its energy from this early life, but I have worked on my art in my fiction, and here, in these pages, I want to discuss the origins of that life and its surroundings. I have always paid close attention to my family history, absorbed every detail of what happened and to whom it happened and when it happened and why it happened and how each person felt about it. All this was extremely important to me, though I can't say exactly why. I don't think my mother cared two hoots about the "old country." It was better forgotten, as far as she was concerned, but I believe that what happened there and how it affected our household is what formed me into the person and writer I became.

My mother had very little use for the immigrant relatives who, with their poor diction, crude thinking, and vulgar behavior, caused her to feel embarrassment and disgust. I don't think my father did much reflecting on the meaning of life (he was too busy trying to earn a living). My grandmother was a peasant woman from Poland, busy cooking and cleaning and grieving her losses on the bench in front of our house. It may have been my aunt, my mother's younger sister, the one who was the wallflower, the one who never left the house, the one who was too delicate to work out in the world, the one who believed she would meet the love of her life, if she was meant to, while putting out the garbage, the one who said my father should have married her and not my mother—it may have been her influence that was so powerful. So little happened to her that she held a magnifying glass to each tiny act that in any way related to her, replayed in her mind every careless remark of a neighbor or relative, relived each gesture of a schoolmate or a girlfriend. She knew all the family tragedies, romances, accidents, suicides, and scandals— and regaled me with their details. She remembered every word some young man or another had ever said to her (or, more to the point, to my mother). She held grudges forever. She remembered slights and rehearsed them every day. She was meticulous in her recollections, particularly if they concerned my mother, who always denied what her sister remembered about her. My aunt saw significance in everything. As did I.

∽∾

My mother's mother, Beckie Panker Sorblum, had come to America in steerage from Kutno, Poland at the age of twenty-one. She was courted by her handsome first husband, Davis Josephthal, who told her that he spoke seven languages and had been an aristocrat in Europe. In fact, he had left a wife and daughter behind in Europe, which he neglected to tell her. He soon abandoned my grandmother, too, and she was forced by circumstance to put her two small children, Eva and Sam, into an orphanage. She found work as a midwife during the years she was going through the formal requirements to attain her *get* (Jewish divorce). When she finally did, she learned that her husband had died in a diabetic coma shortly after leaving her.

Through acquaintances, as was the way in those days, she met my grandfather, a tailor eleven years her junior named Morris Sorblum (although before he passed through Ellis Island his name had been Sauerbach). Soon after their marriage, they had two children: my mother, Jessie Sorblum, born November 28, 1907, and my aunt, Yetta Sorblum, born June 10, 1910. They lived briefly on the Lower East Side of New York, then moved to an apartment at 613 East 138th Street in the Bronx, where they paid a rent of $38 a month for five rooms. My grandfather's employer, who owned a women's garment factory, also owned the apartment house in which the family lived, so that whatever my grandfather earned at work, he paid back to his boss in rent.

The two sisters, Jessie and Yetta, went to P.S. 9, the school where my mother got her first look at the genteel, cultured life of her (gentile) teachers. She aspired to education, to speaking the English language in beautiful tones. She told me many times of her greatest humiliation: when she encountered her first grade teacher in the street, the teacher did not seem to recognize her. My mother said to her, "Oh dear, teacher don't know me." Immediately, she was aware of her grammatical error and was shamed by it. By the passion and frequency with which she told this story, I know she was haunted by this lapse all her life. At graduation from eighth grade, she won the gold medal for academic excellence. As she stood in the darkened audience to go up to the stage to receive her prize, the boy who had been in competition with her for the medal muttered to her as she passed him by, "Just wait till I get you outside." Many Jewish parents, who had left their homes and families and crossed an ocean to seek education and a better life for their offspring, demanded and expected that their children bring home academic honors. (I don't think this was the case in my mother's home, however.) My grandmother Beckie was a mild-mannered, simple person who had no knowledge of book learning or desire for it. If anyone yearned for education, it was my mother. When she was eighty-six years old and living, paralyzed, in a nursing home, she still cherished her gold medal. On the day my daughter Joanna passed her orals in comparative literature at Yale, my mother asked me to give it as a gift to her.

When my mother was seven, her parents noticed that she spent much of her time "playing piano" on the edge of the kitchen table. They arranged to buy her an upright piano and weekly piano lessons. She devoted herself to practicing and was soon playing the music of Chopin, Mozart, and Beethoven. When her mother's parents, Fanny (Feygele) and Israel Panker (Poker), had come to the United States from Poland, they had lived for a time with my grandmother's sister, Sarah Panker Weisgrow. When Fanny took ill, however, she moved into the Bronx apartment to be nursed by my grandmother. Her bed was placed in front of the piano, denying my mother access to her precious hours of practice time. My mother told me she did not have charitable thoughts about the old woman, whose smell was unpleasant and whose bed blocked her way to the piano. Not long after that, my mother was at a party and remembers feeling an icy sensation come over her. She knew something dreadful had happened; when she got home, she learned that her grandmother had died.

My mother's father's parents, David Ichiel and Elka Hyah Sorblum, came to America, too, when their children could arrange to

Merrill's mother, Jessie Sorblum, age thirteen, at eighth-grade graduation wearing a gold medal for academic excellence, circa 1920.

care for them, but my mother could not speak Yiddish (and refused to learn it), so she had almost no communication with them.

In 1924, when my mother and her sister were fourteen and sixteen, the family moved from the Lower East Side to Brooklyn. My aunt told me very recently that the reason for their move was that my mother was ashamed of their living quarters, that, after one of her dates ("a goy") took her home and expressed surprise that she "lived in such a dump," she demanded of my grandfather that they move to a classier place. "She always got what she wanted." The small, two-story house they bought (for $9,999) at 405 Avenue O in Brooklyn was hardly a castle, although I sometimes thought it was; my novel *The Kingdom of Brooklyn* is set in the world of my childhood there.

My grandfather made his living studying the fashions in windows of department stores and then copying them in sample patterns he made for his employer. In his nights at home, he sewed stylish clothes for his daughters. My mother was always proud to be well dressed.

He also had a great love for opera, and especially for the singer Enrico Caruso. Buying the cheapest tickets to the Metropolitan Opera House, he frequently took my mother with him, and together they stood in the back of the theater to watch the performances. On his Victrola at home, he played the great operas and instructed her in the highlights of their melodrama.

At some point my mother was faced with the choice of attending one of two high schools: Hunter, which offered an academic program, or Roosevelt, which offered a commercial course. Because she had a girlfriend going to Roosevelt who begged her to go there, my mother agreed—and, once there, found herself bored and impatient. (As my aunt made clear to me, eager to set the record straight once again, "Your mother thought she knew more than her teachers.")

My mother dropped out of high school and took a brief business course, after which she went to work for a law firm. She got the job by stating that she'd had previous legal experience. On her first day there, when a man came into the office and asked for "the process server," she commenced to look in the drawers of her desk, thinking it must be something like a cake server. (She told this story without amusement; being humiliated as a result of her ignorance was intolerable to her.)

A year after the family moved to the house in Brooklyn, my grandmother's son, Sam Josephthal, was drowned at sea. He had served in the infantry during World War I, and, after the war, he lived with the family in the Brooklyn house, contributing not only a thousand dollars of the two-thousand-dollar down payment but also helping with the mortgage payments. Eva was married by then, to Eddie Sherman, a prizefighter. They also lived in a house in Brooklyn with their three sons: my cousins Irving, Henry, and Fred. As the story was told all the years I was growing up, Sam went fishing one stormy Yom Kippur night in 1925—went fishing with a "bad lot" of friends on a night when a good Jewish son should have been in *shul*—and was lost when his boat sank in the waters off Coney Island.

(Sixty years after his disappearance, my Aunt Eva, sitting with me, in 1985, on the porch of her retirement hotel in Miami Beach, told me the truth that had never been told to my grandmother or my mother or my aunt. Sam's boat had, in fact, been gunned down by the Coast Guard. On that stormy night in the Prohibition year of 1925, he and his friends had been bootlegging whiskey over the high seas.)

After his disappearance, my mother, only eighteen, was required to take on the grisly job of visiting the morgue to look at the faces of drowned men in the hope of identifying her brother. (He was never found, and, seven years later, the family was allowed to collect on his thousand-dollar life insurance policy.)

In 1929, only four years after Sam's drowning, my grandfather, Morris Sorblum, died, on March 15, at the age of forty-eight. His death was due to suffocation brought on by the swelling of the floor of his mouth. His severe throat pain had been misdiagnosed over the phone by a neighborhood doctor who dismissed it as a "only a sore throat" and refused to make a house call. My mother called him a second time, in desperation, when my grandfather claimed that his pain was so severe he was going to throw himself out the window The doctor said my grandfather was "just high strung and of a nervous temperament" and "tended to exaggerate." My mother finally called for an ambulance. As they carried my grandfather down the stairs, he looked at my mother, who was standing at the foot of the stairs, just outside the door. When he passed by her, he admonished her to "button up your coat." He died in the ambulance on the way to the hospital.

His illness was later identified as Ludwig's angina, a disease that was often fatal before the advent of antibiotics. After his death (on March 15, which would be the date of my birth nine years later), my mother called the local doctor who had refused to come to see her father. She threatened to kill him. Within weeks, she told me, he had closed his practice and moved out of the neighborhood.

My grandmother, who had a poor command of English (she spoke mainly Yiddish), was faced with finding a way to pay off the mortgage. My mother was already working. Her sister, Yetta, who in high school had changed her name to Yvonne, then to Yvette, and, finally, to Greta, began to bake cookies at home and to box them for my mother to take with her to her office building in Manhattan to sell to fellow workers. My mother told me she hated carrying greasy cardboard boxes (the grease stained the fine clothes that her father had sewn for her). My mother by then was earning $41 a week, an unusually high salary for those times, and was working for two New York state senators, Elwood M. Raybenold and Charles E. Scribner. So impressed were they with her competence and intelligence that they offered to send her to law school at night while she continued to work for them during the day. She was flattered and considered the offer seriously but finally had to decline. There were not enough hours in the day and night to do all she would have had to do.

In 1933, my Aunt Greta gave a party at the Brooklyn house, to which my father came along (or more likely was dragged along) as the buddy of one of my aunt's friends. He was brought, the story goes, as the "date" for my aunt. Uneasy in the crowd of strangers in the house, he wandered out to the front porch and sat there alone in the dark, smoking his pipe. This is where he first saw my mother, who was coming home from a date with a young lawyer. I've heard many versions of this meeting, and it was one of my earliest inspirations—and the basis for "How Love Came to Grandmother" in my first book of stories, *Stop Here, My Friend*—for using family history in my fiction.

My parents married on November 10, 1934, in a wedding that took place in the house on Avenue O. (My father's mother was against this marriage, believing that her three sons should not marry before their two sisters were married. Neither of my father's sisters seemed destined to make an early marriage, and eventually all the brothers took wives while "the girls" were still single.)

My mother and father, as newlyweds, lived on in the house with my aunt and grandmother. (My parents were given the large upstairs front bedroom, while my grandmother and my aunt shared a bed in the back bedroom.) My father took upon himself the duties of supporting my grandmother and aunt (my mother continued to work, as well) and did whatever work came his way. His first job was as a sales clerk in the men's pajama department of Loeser's Department Store.

My father's history, like my mother's, was about struggle and survival. His mother, Fanny Goldstein Gerber, had five children: Lillian, Nat, William (this was my father's American name, but he was called *Velvel Gerber* in elementary school, and sometimes *Meyer Wolf*), Mac, and Pauline. Fanny had to accept the charity of her brother, Harry Goldstein, after her husband, my paternal grandfather, Abraham Gerber—so the story goes—was hit on the head by a falling hammer while working in the navy yards, an accident that left him not quite "right in the head" afterward. I never met him, nor did my mother, although she often packed boxes of goodies and sweets for my father and his brothers to bring to him when they went off on Sunday afternoons to visit him in what must have been the insane asylum. (None of the brothers and sisters would ever discuss his illness with me, not then and not when I was an adult.)

My grandmother Fanny lived upstairs in her brother Harry Goldstein's house on 86th Street in Bensonhurst; Harry ran a profitable neighborhood liquor store with his brothers. Only my father's eldest brother, Nat, was given (or took for himself) the opportunity to go to college. He later became rich and successful in the oil business and moved to Park Avenue in Manhattan, where he and his wife, Bertha, and their children, Iris and Eddie, lived in high style.

Each of the other Gerber siblings made his way as best he could. None of them, I think, aside from my Uncle Nat, finished high school. I know my father did not even finish sixth grade.

After he married my mother, he plunged into one business venture after another. In 1936, he traveled to Cleveland with her to look into a business venture he'd heard was promising: servicing crane machines and pinball machines in bars and roadhouses. The crane machine was actually a form of gambling. It had a claw hand that reached into a pile of "prizes" each time a player deposited a coin. Occasionally the claw would grasp a toy, a cheap wrist watch, or some other object, and drop it into a chute, from which it would slide out to the patron. People seemed to love playing these machines, and my father had high hopes for the business. He planned to set up a series of them in New York, but they were destined to be pronounced illegal by Governor Thomas Dewey, who ordered that all crane machines in the city be dumped into the East River.

My mother wrote letters home from Cleveland, testifying to the rare pleasure of being alone with my father. On November 10, 1936, their second anniversary, she wrote:

> Dear Mom and Gretch—Your lovely card duly arrived. . . . Will brought me a lovely one & a grand corsage of gardenias. We went to see the only show in town, Naughty Marietta—orchestra—tenth row. . . . After we left Will drove home in what seemed a strange direction, and then pulled up in a sinister looking block with Negroes all over the place. I hadn't expected to be taken anywhere else, but there we were at Cedar Gardens, the Cotton Club of Cleveland. It was a strange and nice experience . . . a really nice place, all Negro entertainers and mighty good ones. We stayed for two floor shows—both different—and got home at 3. . . . Anyhow, we had a grand a glorious evening—and I know you'll be glad.

In another letter written home to Brooklyn, February 25, 1937, my mother says, "Maybe I'll do some work on my scrap book this afternoon. Though I have some silk underwear needs ironing . . . and Will's shorts need sewing together. . . . Soon my Willyum will be home . . . so long now while I beautify myself."

Merrill on the beach in wartime, as soldiers stand in a mess-hall line in the background, Miami Beach, 1943.

This period away was one of the few times my parents spent alone for the next fifteen years. I was conceived in Cleveland and born in Brooklyn on March 15, 1938.

⟨∞⟩

My father, always willing to try again, began to work on a series of inventions. He perfected (or so he thought), among other things, a

In the house of her father's uncle, Harry Goldstein: Merrill's father, Merrill (age five), mother, grandmother Beckie Sorblum, and Aunt Greta, 1944.

wooden hockey game with twirling hockey sticks, a plastic device called "Stand-a-Plate" (which didn't stand up—all the plates tipped over and broke), and in the fifties he wanted to take a patent on a Coney Island-type ride called "The Merry-Go-Bob"—named for myself and my sister, Barbara.

In 1943, my father and mother decided to leave my grandmother and my aunt in Brooklyn for a few months and to take a trip to Miami Beach, a place where my father had always dreamed of living. It was wartime; soldiers were on the beach and occupying most of the hotels. My father opened a small business cutting records for soldiers who, before they shipped out, wanted to send messages home to their wives and mothers.

My mother found herself pregnant during this time, and it was also in these months in Florida that we learned (from a newspaper my mother opened one morning and in which she read the "Missing in Action" list) about the disappearance of Henry, my Aunt

Merrill, age four, with cousin Henry Sherman, "The Lost Airman," Brooklyn, 1942.

Eva's middle son (who was born exactly—to the day—twenty years before I was, on March 15, 1918). He had always wanted to be a flier and had enlisted in the air force to train as a pilot. While he was in training, he wrote home often, sending pictures of himself in flight gear to his mother and little presents for me. I still have his gold air force wings. (This story is told in the essay "The Lost Airman.")

Merrill's father in his store at 33 Hansen Place, Brooklyn, circa 1946.

My sister, Barbara, was born near the war's end, on February 17, 1945. My father opened an antique shop at 33 Hansen Place, Brooklyn. He stocked it, to begin with, with the contents of a trunk he bought at an auction. He called the store Gerber's Jewelry Exchange (later Gerber's Antiques), and it became the source—under one guise or another—of our family's income from that time on.

In our house on Avenue O, my Aunt Greta, who had learned beauty skills by assisting a neighborhood beautician named Edith Lee, opened a small beauty shop in an upstairs bedroom. Women came and went all day. I often sat nearby as she cut hair and filed nails and listened to the women tell the stories of their lives.

When I was ten, my grandmother, who was then seventy-seven, seemed to take a sudden turn for the worse. Coming home from school, I would often find a doctor at her side, treating her for spasms of chest pain, dizziness, and shortness of breath. My aunt and my mother leaned over her, waiting to see whether she would live or die. Their anxiety indicated to me constantly (as if I hadn't already noticed this) that life was a dangerous and ultimately fatal business. Likewise, when my father was late coming home (he often went on "calls" to buy antiques for his store), my mother, aunt, and grandmother would watch out the window for his car, conjecturing about whether he'd been shot in a holdup, killed in a car accident on

Merrill and Aunt Greta, Brooklyn, 1944.

the icy streets, or abducted for ransom. I went to sleep on many nights expecting never to see my father again.

On the other hand, my father had a genial, relaxed nature and a supreme talent for enjoying life. When he wasn't working, he sat in the sun smoking his pipe, or played with the dog, or went fishing. I was always aware that the women in my life regarded this playful enjoyment of life as foolish and irresponsible: to be anxious and to be

Merrill, age seven, at 405 Avenue O, Brooklyn.

worried were the only important acts of existence; the rest was time wasted.

I am told I rarely smiled as a child. At some point, my mother, who composed coy jingles and rhyming verse nearly every day of her life, wrote a note and left it at my place at the table: "If smiles she won't hoard, I'm pretty sure she'll get a reward!" I was insulted and humiliated by the criticism, and not at all amused.

I discovered early that reading books was the best way to find out what life was really about. Like Saul Bellow, who said that "fiction is news from existence," I found that fiction told me more about truth than truth did. Fiction was the telling of secrets. From fiction I learned about romantic love, about passion, about the details of childbirth. I learned that life was not, for everyone, exactly as it took place in my house. Such revelations gave me hope for my own future. Books also provided a retreat from the noisy, intrusive demands of a crowded household.

The first television set did not arrive in my neighborhood till I was twelve years old—and, when I went to a neighbor's house to watch it, most often I saw Milton Berle cavorting about in a dress! I was always glad to return to my books.

My father used to take me to the Brooklyn public library every Friday evening, and I'd come home with a huge armful of books. Because he also bought out "estates" for his antique business, he often brought home cartons of books for me, and I'd arrange them in tall piles beside my bed. The "best" books were at the bottom, to be saved for last. These were Nancy Drew mysteries and books about collies. I made a rule for myself that I had to read all the books, even the ones about the Civil War and medical diseases. I didn't have to read *all* of every book, but I had to give each one a fair chance. I got up an hour early to read before school. Sometimes there were duplicates; my father always urged me to give the extra book away to a friend. He didn't understand that two books were twice the treasure; also, that I had no worthy friends.

My mother had an affinity for only one book: the dictionary. She spent hours teaching me to rhyme. Her vocabulary was exceptional, her typing skills superb, and as always she spent hours at the piano. Sometimes she played songs to which my father sang along ("Sewanee River," "White Christmas," "Danny Boy"), though she generally felt it was beneath her to be an "accompanist" or to play "popular" music. I was not inclined to enjoy piano lessons much myself but found myself fascinated by the typewriter keyboard and, in fact,

Merrill, age thirteen, on the day of her eighth-grade graduation, in the garden at 405 Avenue O, with her sister, Barbara; her mother; and her father, 1951.

won the typing medal at my high school graduation. The pleasure of writing, for me, still includes the pleasure of typing.

The first poems I wrote were about the women who came to my aunt's beauty parlor: "My aunt has a customer, her name is Sadie, I like her very very much, for she is a nice lady." In the same series was this poem: "I have a friend Allen, Scarlet Fever he has, he likes music very much, especially jazz." In 1951, when I was thirteen, a boy from my class invited me to the movies, and I still have the manuscript of the story I wrote, called "First Date." One passage reads: "I was in the middle of my top lip when the doorbell rang. There went my lipstick, down my chin."

Around this time, I (undoubtedly with my mother's help) wrote a jingle that was published in my eighth-grade school magazine at P.S 238. It began:

> Seven A.M. the alarm starts in beepin'
> And I start to think "What a swell day for sleepin'" —

Hurry and eat, get dressed on the double,
If I am late there'll be plenty of trouble."

I don't think my heart was ever in any of these "cute" efforts. My mother, who had a strong penchant for rhyme, oversaw and directed my creative output, which clearly expressed more of my mother's talents than mine. She excelled at singsong rhymes and wrote skits for the PTA and the Girl Scouts (some of her rhymes were set to music and performed at my school), and she published amusing verse in the local newspapers. I came across one she wrote in 1966, which is titled "Supermarket" and begins:

My confusion is great
I fear for my fate
My marketing's become such a chore,
One needs a degree
At least Ph.D.
To cope with the problems past that door.

I was embarrassed by her flip facility, and, besides, I had darker thoughts, more ominous things than she had (or was willing to express) to write about.

In 1952, when I was fourteen and my sister seven, my parents moved to Miami Beach and left my aunt and my grandmother behind in the house in Brooklyn. (In 1949, my aunt had married Alex Mitchell, a cabinetmaker, who had three grown children from a previous marriage.) My sister and I had been sick so often during the bitter winters (I had pneumonia four times before I was fourteen) that a doctor recommended to my parents that they consider moving with us to a milder climate. My father, who had always wanted to live in Florida, was eager to move, and my mother finally felt able to break away from her mother and her sister. She craved, and was going to get, at long last, some privacy and a life of her own with her family.

I started tenth grade at Miami Beach High School and joined a Young Judea club whose leader made a great impression on me. I had a new nickname now—of all things, "Merry"—and I arrived in Florida ready to live a transformed life. From the gray skies of

Brooklyn, I now looked out upon the pastel blues and greens of ocean and palm trees. My parents were in high spirits for a short time, having hopes, once again, for success in business. I started tenth grade at Miami Beach High School, so different from the dangerous high school I'd gone to in ninth grade, where so many of the young Italian boys carried switchblades. In the new school, whose students were mostly Jewish, there was an innocence and an air of cheerful trust in the world and in the future. Of course, these were the naive "fifties"—we believed we'd encounter no obstacles as we made our way into the future.

However, almost at once, my father trusted the wrong man and lost our family's fortune. My mother was furious with him; she had to get a job as a typist to keep a roof over our heads. Their hostility did not make life simple, living as we did, the four of us, in a one-bedroom apartment.

I was writing quite a bit then, partly to escape the confines of our small quarters and partly to explore the new emotions I was feeling. Many of my early stories were deeply romantic, if not totally sentimental. (One story I recall from this period was about two palm trees that grew side by side and that were downed in a hurricane. When the storm subsided, it was discovered that—wonder of wonders—their roots were intertwined!)

In Miami Beach, which my parents felt was a "safe place," I was free to take the bus downtown to the library near the ocean, and there I sometimes met my new classmates from the high school. (It was in the stacks of this library that I encountered my first flasher.) The novels I'd read had taught me that fiction was permitted to contain secrets that could never be spoken of. This freedom, possible only in writing, was, or could be, one of the few freedoms I could claim. I decided I would write my own stories; I would tell the secrets of my heart.

I met my future husband, Joseph Spiro, when I was fifteen: this event is recorded in my diary as follows:

Sunday, March 7, 1954: Today I went on a Young Judea picnic . . . this one is only a week and a day away from my birthday. I met the leader . . . and he is as wonderful as Irma says. He makes you like him the minute you meet him. The boys were the same as usual, but I got to talking with Joe Spiro and he is very nice . . . he stayed with me most of the time and when they played ball he knew I didn't want to play, so he offered to take a walk with me.

Just days later, I saw Joe waiting for a bus outside the hole-in-the-wall store my father had rented in the lobby of the Roberts Hotel on Flagler Street in downtown Miami and where he conducted (for a time, till the inevitable failure caused him to move on) a watch-repair business. I would sometimes go there with him on Saturdays and help him wind the watches. It was outside this store that Joe Spiro waited each week to take a bus to his piano lesson. (A pianist! How this would please my mother, I thought.) I eventually loaned him a book of duets and suggested that one day we play together. Later, I wrote in my diary: "What a woman won't do for a man!"

The diary was a grand thing my father had given me while we were still in Brooklyn—a book as big in size as the edition of *Gone with the Wind* I had read when I was thirteen, a printer's dummy bound in gray cloth with the title on the spine announcing *The Heritage of the Bounty*. On the front of the book was an engraving of an old sailing ship with its sails raised and engorged with wind. Inside my father had written, "To Merry, a book to enter happy & interesting events, Dad." (In my eighth-grade autograph book, he had written, "Look up, aim high, you'll get there by and by.")

Writing in this diary gave me the sense that I was actually writing a book. On April 24, 1954, I entered this note: "Well, at least if I don't ever write a book I can say I did. This could sort of be called my autobiography." On a prior page I had written, "I hate Chemistry and Gym. School is getting to be a pain. It's raining now. I wonder if I'm like Emily Dickinson. After I die this whole book may be published. God forbid!! Oh well—back to my term paper."

At some level, I already saw myself as a writer. I filled the whole diary (and spent much of my time hiding it from my sister). The ecstasies and disappointments recorded therein are cause for embarrassment now, but at the time there were matters so serious and so private going on that I wrote about them in shorthand (which I was learning at the time; every girl of my generation was advised, indeed,

Merrill, age seventeen, with Joe Spiro, Miami Beach, 1955.

commanded, to take typing and shorthand). Of course, I can no longer decipher those entries now.

(The habit of diary writing, which developed into the more serious form of journal keeping and later included the recording of all my dreams, became a daily habit of my life. To date I have filled fifteen manuscript boxes with typewritten journal entries and have also recorded thousands of dreams, from the early 1950s on. The comfort of wrapping words around thoughts and images is pleasure, necessity, and sustenance for me.)

When Joe Spiro graduated from high school in 1954, he went to college at the University of Florida in Gainesville, four hundred miles to the north of Miami. I planned to follow him there the next year, when I was to graduate. Unfortunately, and to my dismay, I won a scholarship to the University of Miami and found myself, at the beginning of my freshman year, starting college there, miserable about being separated from Joe. College for girls in the mid-1950s was a questionable experience, in any case. Though we were not consciously aware of the oppressiveness of the times as we lived through them (it's astonishing now how much abuse one is willing to accept as "necessary"), freshman girls who lived in the dormitories were treated virtually as prison inmates. Girls had to be in by 9:00 P.M., and a flashlight check was made every night to certify that each girl was in her proper bed.

I had registered to take a writing class with Fred Shaw, a popular teacher and a columnist for the Miami *Herald* who held his class in the evening in a local coffee shop. In order for me to get permission to be out after 9:00 P.M., I had to petition the dean of women students and beg for the privilege to take the class. All freshmen were required to wear little beanies and to obey orders of upperclassmen. Any infraction of these silly rules would bring upon one a summons to "Honor Court." Punishment for breaking a rule required hours of service doing ridiculous things. I had no heart for this, especially when I was stopped and "arrested" for not wearing my beanie and told I had to appear in court for a "trial." I broke down in tears more than once when talking on the phone to my parents. I begged to be allowed to go to the University of Florida. They couldn't fail to recognize how miserable I was, and they did understand how badly I wanted to be with Joe. Finally, they agreed that I could transfer to the state college at the end of the term.

In February 1956, I triumphantly took what was called the "milk train" to Ocala, Florida, where Joe Spiro met me at the station. There, in Gainesville, in the beautiful university environment of the north Florida woods, I had the good fortune to meet the great writing teacher of my life, Andrew Lytle. One of the original Agrarians at Vanderbilt University and a close friend of Allen Tate, Lytle was then just finishing his novel, *The Velvet Horn*. His workshop had (and still has) legendary standing. It was in his class that I first understood I had a serious calling. He taught the stories of his favorite writers, among them James Joyce, Flannery O'Connor, and Katherine Anne Porter. (This experience is described in my essay "Follow the Thread into the Labyrinth: A Fond Recollection of Andrew Lytle.")

By the time I left the University of Florida and entered Brandeis University as a graduate student, I was certain I would have a life as a writer. Only a few universities at that time actually had departments of creative writing, Stanford and Iowa being the main ones. I had earlier applied to the Iowa Writing Program with a letter of reference from Andrew Lytle, and, although I had received an invitation from Paul Engle, his offer was too small ($300) to take me very far. My parents were against the idea of my going to so cold and so far away a place as Iowa. Besides, Joe Spiro was at Brandeis, and that's where I truly wanted to be.

While a student at Brandeis, I fulfilled the requirements for a master's degree in English, taking courses in Samuel Johnson, in Robert Frost, in Whitman and Dickinson, in D. H. Lawrence. I remember my shock at how backward I seemed and how lacking my education appeared when the first professor I encountered asked us to list the names of five well-known literary critics. I didn't know one name. Some of my classmates, having done their undergraduate work at Ivy League colleges, could easily reel off a list. My second major embarrassment concerned the title I gave to the master's paper I wrote on Samuel Johnson: I called it "The Friendly Giant." And, if I am not mistaken, I turned in the paper I wrote on Emily Dickinson fastened with a pink ribbon. Even so, my professor, Milton

Hindus, told me I had delivered to him one of the best Dickinson papers he had ever received. In like manner, he offered considerable praise for my paper on D. H. Lawrence's "The Fox."

Still, I was not really cut out to be a scholar. Whenever I could find time (sometimes even in class itself), I wrote stories, many of which dealt with my recently completed teenage years. I submitted these stories to popular magazines for young women and to one in particular called *Datebook* magazine. To my delight, an editor named Art Unger began to buy and to publish them. At this time, I also acquired a New York agent, Sterling Lord. One snowy day, I went to New York to meet him so that we could discuss "my career strategy." He encouraged me to continue writing teen stories and eventually sold many of these stories to *Datebook* for $100 each (with a 10 percent commission for himself). Toward the end of my first year at Brandeis, having completed the course work for the M.A. degree (but not having taken the orals), I applied for a fellowship to go on toward the Ph.D. Irving Howe, then the head of the Brandeis English Department, spoke to me about my application: he told me, in so many words, that I was "only a girl and only a writer" and that, although I had grades and qualifications good enough to receive one of the department's fellowships, there were men he felt needed them more than I did. The year was 1960; men were still unselfconscious about making remarks of this kind to women. Howe's clear dismissal (of my sex, of my talent, and of me) took care of my hopes for staying on in graduate school. After my conversation with him, I decided not to take my oral exams. I expected I would fail, and I didn't wish to be further humiliated.

(Twenty years later, in 1981, I appealed to Brandeis University for the opportunity to complete my degree. With the intervention of my professor, Milton Hindus, it was arranged that I would take the M.A. written exam [orals were no longer required for the master's degree] at a college in California where the exam could be monitored. I did, in fact, write a three-hour exam on the subject "How is *To the Lighthouse* a book about growing up?" I passed and received my master's degree.)

In 1961, however, after I left Brandeis, my life took another direction. Since Joe Spiro and I were planning to marry (which we had done, on June 23, 1960), I began looking for a job in the Boston environs where we planned to live while he stayed on at Brandeis working on his degree in the history of ideas. (Our first apartment was in an attic at 14½ Prentiss Street, Cambridge.) I was hired as an editorial assistant by Houghton Mifflin Publishers and spent a year working in the educational department on Tremont Street but frequently making visits to the trade offices at 2 Park Street, where the "real writing" (poetry and fiction) was being read and edited. Philip Roth had just published *Goodbye, Columbus* with Houghton Mifflin, and I read and reread his collection, marveling at his brutal honesty in writing about family life. I think he gave me courage to take certain risks in my work, although I was already well on my way to alienating my relatives even at that time.

During that year at Houghton Mifflin, I sat at my desk at a window that overlooked the golden dome of the State House and the green expanse of Boston Commons, and I imagined the stories I wanted to write. Since my husband was applying to various colleges for a job for the following fall, I also applied for something new and promising: a Wallace Stegner fiction fellowship at Stanford University in California. We had no clear sense of where the future would take us: we were open to all possibilities.

Just as in some of my duller college lecture classes I sometimes wrote stories in my notebook instead of taking class notes, that year at Houghton Mifflin, on lunch hours and on days when there was not much work, I managed to make notes for a story or two. I finished one story called "The Cost Depends on What You Reckon It In," which was about an old woman in a Brooklyn nursing home. (My grandmother had been in such a home.) Written from the point of view of the old woman's daughter who visits her three times a day, the story (as it turned out) proved to be an exploration of the subject of old age, which I was to treat extensively in much of my later work.

My agent, Sterling Lord, who had been selling my teen stories to *Datebook,* wrote me after he read it that I'd best stick to what worked, and he urged me not to write this sort of story, which he described to me as "maudlin."

Outraged (an emotion I have experienced a good deal in my many years of having my work rejected), I decided to dismiss my agent. I did so and went ahead and submitted the story on my own to *Mademoiselle* magazine. Just at that time, I was called on by my employer to account for some error regarding a piece used in one of Houghton Mifflin's anthologies for which proper acknowledgment had not been made. The anthology, which I had edited, had previously been worked on by a former employee, who, as far as I understood the situation, had made the original error. Still, the repercussions at the publishing house were serious (was there a lawsuit threatened?), and the result was that I was dismissed from a job I didn't care for all that much. As fortune would have it, during my very first week out of work, I received a letter from *Mademoiselle* offering to buy my story "The Cost Depends on What You Reckon It In." Jubilant, I realized that I was the real thing: an unemployed writer. Furthermore, *Mademoiselle* was famous for publishing the early works of many great writers. I was on my way.

And there was another piece of news, as well. I learned, just about that time, that I was going to be a mother! Then—more news! Just days before our daughter, Becky Ann Spiro, was to be born, I got the telegram announcing that I had won a Wallace Stegner Fellowship at Stanford University in California! (My experience at Stanford is described in the essay "Wallace Stegner and the Stanford Writing Workshop.")

After our year at Stanford, Joe and I spent two years in Riverside, California, where Joe taught history at the University of California at Riverside. On January 17, 1965, our second daughter, Joanna Emily Spiro, was born. Joe accepted a job teaching history at Pasadena City College, and we moved to Monterey Park, California.

My parents and Joe's parents had moved to California from Florida by then, and it seemed we were situated for life now in the west. In 1965, my first book of stories, *Stop Here, My Friend,* was published by Houghton Mifflin (the same publishing house that had fired me in 1961), and I was invited to teach writing at the University of Redlands, in Redlands, California, in the fall of the year. In August 1965, my father was diagnosed with lymphocytic leukemia. In his brief period of remission, because he didn't want me to have to drive a long distance alone, he drove with me once a week from Monterey Park to Redlands, where he waited while I taught my class. My father died at

Merrill, with Stegner Fellows Ed McClanahan and, sitting behind him, Robert Stone, Stanford University, 1963.

Merrill and Joe with their daughters Susanna (three months), Joanna (two years), and Becky (five years), Monterey Park, California, 1967.

the age of fifty-six on December 7, 1965. (For seventeen more years, my mother continued to run the antiques store, Gerber's Antiques, on Melrose Avenue, in Los Angeles, that she and my father had opened in 1963.)

Two of my books of fiction, *Anna in Chains* and *Anna in the After-life,* follow my mother through the various circumstances of her widowhood.

From the time of my first sale to *Redbook* in 1962, I understood that it was possible to write, in many different tones, the family stories that interested me. "A Daughter of My Own," published in 1964, was the first of a series of "lighter" stories that I wrote for *Redbook* over the next twenty-seven years. In these stories, Janet and Danny and their three daughters travel through the arc of family life, from the time before the birth of the first child to the day the youngest goes away to college and beyond, when Janet and Danny are once again alone with each other.

After we moved to Monterey Park, my third daughter, Susanna Willa Spiro, was born, on May 1, 1967. In the years that I was home with my three little girls, all born within a five-year period, writing these stories kept me sane and challenged. Women of my generation raising children in the sixties did not, in general, go to work. *Redbook* welcomed my interpretation of American motherhood and the adventures of family life and paid me generously. A first sale in those days of the early sixties brought a thousand dollars. (I believe that's still about what they pay now, thirty years later.) I stress that the stories were "American"—meaning that any specific rendition of Jewish family life was definitely not welcome. "Ethnic" fiction was not being written (or was, but was not readily published) in those days. More than once, I was asked to remove something particularly Jewish, even if it was only a Jewish-sounding name. I published stories not only in *Redbook* in the sixties and throughout the decades that followed but also in the *New Yorker* (two of my stories were published there in the early sixties, but none were accepted after my editor, Rachel MacKenzie, died), in the *Ladies' Home Journal,* in *Family Circle,* in *Good Housekeeping,* in *McCall's,* and in *Woman's Day.* During the same period, my "literary" stories were accepted by the *Virginia Quarterly Review,* the *Sewanee Review,* the *Atlantic,*

Thanksgiving at Merrill's house: Merrill's mother, sister Barbara, Merrill, Merrill's daughters Joanna and Becky, and Aunt Greta, Sierra Madre, California, 1987.

Shenandoah, Prairie Schooner, and other quarterlies. A number of these stories won prizes, including "At the Fence," which won the Andrew Lytle Fiction Prize for the best story in the *Sewanee Review* in 1985, and "I Don't Believe This," first published in the *Atlantic* and chosen for *The O. Henry Prize Stories: 1986.*

Eventually, I sold *Redbook* forty-two stories (I was told I hold the record for having sold more stories to *Redbook* than any other author), and, in 1993, Longstreet Press published a collection of twenty-five related stories about Janet and Danny, titled *This Old Heart of Mine: The Best of Merrill Joan Gerber's Redbook Stories.*

Not until I was described in a review as a "women's magazine" writer did I ever see myself in this light. Just as when I spoke to my children I used a manner of speaking appropriate to their ages, so would I write in a mode appropriate to the level of my purpose and intent. (Cynthia Ozick once remarked of me that I have "many arrows in my quiver.") I have learned, from hard experience, that the literary world does not think well of a writer who publishes in popular magazines. In 1967, when my novel *An Antique*

Merrill with Andrew Lytle (left) and Smith Kirkpatrick at an event honoring Andrew Lytle, De Kalb College, Georgia, 1989.

Man was published by Houghton Mifflin, *Time* magazine sent a photographer to my home. He stayed all day, had me serve him lunch, asked me to change my clothing three times, and led me to believe that *Time* intended to cover my book in a serious way. Cover it they did (they ran a review but used no photograph), and the phrase I remember all these years later is the reviewer's remark to the effect that "Gerber, who writes for the women's magazines, makes it all come out right in the end."

For the past twenty-five years, I have applied for Guggenheim grants and NEA grants but have received neither. As an agent once told me, "You fall between the stools," and, indeed, I believe that a writer is taken less seriously if she writes in different voices and modes. In the early 1980s, my friend and correspondent Norma Klein suggested that I write for young adult readers since I knew intimately the voices and souls of teenagers. In that decade, I wrote nine novels for teenagers.

Merrill; Cynthia Ozick with husband Bernie Hallote; Merrill's daughters Susanna and Joanna; Joanna's fiancé, Ron Katwan, between them; and Joe Spiro at the Ribalow Award ceremony, given by *Hadassah* magazine, for *The Kingdom of Brooklyn,* New York, 1993.

From the time of my first published work in 1956, I have written steadily and published stories or books every year. I teach from time to time at writers' conferences and in 1980 began teaching a class in fiction writing at Pasadena City College, where I taught for ten years. In 1981, I spent a month at Yaddo Writers' Colony in Saratoga Springs, New York. (My time at Yaddo is described in the essay "A Month in the Country at Yaddo.") In 1989, I accepted a position as lecturer in creative writing at the California Institute of Technology, where I still teach.

In looking back over these years of being a writer, I have a sense that my "formative years" came to a close, in a literal sense, after my years in the Stegner workshop. Before that time, the elements of my life were busy arranging themselves into the formula that was to

Merrill and Joe at Santa Monica Pier, California, 1992.

Merrill and her daughters—Susanna, Becky, and Joanna—at Joanna's wedding, 1994.

turn me into a writer. After becoming a "grownup"—a wife and mother who settled in one place—I simply pursued my calling, continuing to observe, to think, to write. My other literary history, of publishers and agents, of triumphs and disappointments, of acceptances and rejections, is quite another story, perhaps one to be told at another time.

What I do see from this vantage point is that certain patterns have emerged that should not (but sometimes do) seem surprising. Though I always knew I was a Jewish girl from Brooklyn, I never defined myself as "a Jewish writer"—perhaps because I never had a Jewish teacher, mentor, or model who encouraged me to stake my claim, or perhaps because I did not live in any formal Jewish community. Fate conspired to have me study the literature of the South (in the South) with Andrew Lytle and the literature of the West (in the West) with Wallace Stegner.

Merrill and Adam, Joanna's son, 1999.

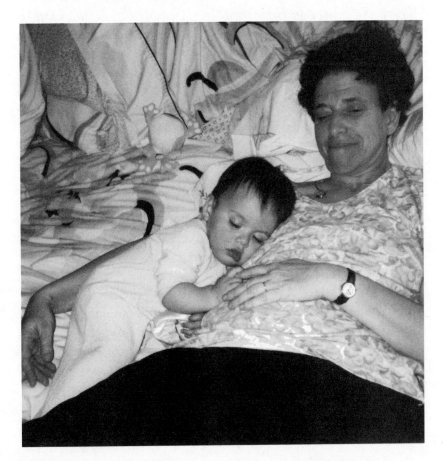

Merrill and Jacob, Becky's son, 2001

However, my sense of myself as a Jewish writer was forcefully confirmed when I received, for my novel *The Kingdom of Brooklyn,* in 1993, the Harold U. Ribalow Prize, given by Hadassah magazine "for literary excellence for a work of fiction on a Jewish theme" (and whose judges were Elie Wiesel, Anne Roiphe, and Louis Begley). This prize, and the Editors' Book Award bestowed on *King of the World* in 1989 by Bill Henderson, of Pushcart Press, "to celebrate an important and unusual book of literary distinction," has been a support to stand against when the tides of rejection (the given of any writer's life) come in hard and strong. My two more recent books of fiction, *Anna in Chains,* and *Anna in the Afterlife,* give voice to the life and struggles of an old Jewish woman who lives alone in the Fairfax area of Los Angeles. My memoir, *Old Mother, Little Cat: A Writer's Reflections on Her Kitten, Her Aged Mother, . . . and Life"* is about my mother's last years in a nursing home. I am never asked now to make my stories "less Jewish" (although an agent did tell me not so long ago to "put a little sunshine in your typewriter").

I have made my home in California; Joe and I live in Sierra Madre in the house we bought thirty-four years ago, near the foothills of the San Gabriel mountains. Our daughters are followers "of the book" (one daughter has a library degree, and two have graduate degrees in literature). Joe and I now have two grandsons, the sons of Becky and Joanna, who have introduced us to a new and extraordinary chapter of our history.

Have I written even a semblance of my autobiography in these pages? As Wallace Stegner suggested, a writer's autobiography occurs regularly in his fiction. The facts, as we remember them, are not always as they were, and, in many cases, after we shape them to our artistic ends, we lose the "truth" entirely. I think the advantage is that we may emerge with a greater truth. I have used my own "facts of life" in my work in many ways, and I have told many stories in many voices. Which story is the true story? Which voice is the true voice? I don't think the writer could begin to tell you the answer.